William Pitt Lennox

Plays, Players and Playhouses at Home and Abroad

With Anecdotes of the Drama and the Stage

William Pitt Lennox

Plays, Players and Playhouses at Home and Abroad
With Anecdotes of the Drama and the Stage

ISBN/EAN: 9783744696364

Printed in Europe, USA, Canada, Australia, Japan

Cover: Foto ©Thomas Meinert / pixelio.de

More available books at **www.hansebooks.com**

PLAYS, PLAYERS, AND PLAYHOUSES
AT HOME AND ABROAD.

VOL. II.

CHAPTER XI.

The French Stage — Jodelle — La Harpe — His Chequered Career—His Tragedies—"The Earl of Warwick"—"Melanie"—"Barmecides"—"Joan of Naples"—"Menzikoff" 159

CHAPTER XII.

The perfection of Tragedy described by Aristotle—La Harpe's Criticisms — Corneille — Voltaire — Pensions granted by Louis XIV. to men of Science and Literature—M. Capelle's remarks on Shakespeare and Addison—Akenside on the genius of Shakespeare 165

CHAPTER XIII.

French Comedy—Molière—Le Sage—Quirault –Brueys—Regnard — Dancourt — Saint Foix — Diderot — Sedaine — Destouches—Boissy—Fabre D'Eglantine . . . 180

CHAPTER XIV.

Duels of Actors—George Garrick, brother to David Garrick, and Baddeley—J. P. Kemble and Aikin—Roselle and Ribou—Fleury and Dugazon—Larive and Florence—Talma and Naudet—Actresses equally Pugnacious—Mesdemoiselles Beaupré and Catherine des Urlis—Mesdemoiselles Theodore and Beaumesuil—Mademoiselle Maupin's rencontre with M. Dumesnil—Inebriety—Mademoiselle Laguerre—Iphigénie en "Champagne," pas en Aulide—Other bibacious Artists—Puffing Advertisements—Realistic Stage effects 193

CHAPTER XV.

French Dramatists unsuccessful when Attempting to Delineate English manners—English Actors at the Porte St. Martin—Talma—Le Kain—Mademoiselle Mars—Dramatic Censor—Hector Malet—Criticism on the English Drama and English Artists 209

CONTENTS.

CHAPTER XVI.
"The Rambler's" opinion of Miss Smithson—Berlioz—His Devotion to the Beautiful Artist—An ill-fated Marriage—"Hands, not hearts" 230

CHAPTER XVII.
Talma in "Britannicus"—Mademoiselle Georges as the Empress Agrippina — French Patriotism — Marshal Ney — Pièces de Circonstance—Fulsome Compliments . 242

CHAPTER XVIII.
Celebrities I have known—Mesdemoiselles Bourgoin, Duchesnois, and Déjazet—LeontineVolny—Leontine Fay, her nom du Théâtre—Romance of real life 249

CHAPTER XIX.
French Managers adopt the system of English Strolling Managers of changing the titles of Plays—Technologie Théâtrale, or Green-room Phraseology 257

PLAYS, PLAYERS, AND PLAYHOUSES.

CHAPTER I.

ANECDOTES OF ELLISTON—A ROYAL VISIT TO DRURY LANE THEATRE—LORD GRAHAM AND THE LESSEE—A CHALLENGE—"ALL'S WELL THAT ENDS WELL"—CRUSADE AGAINST THE MINOR THEATRES—HEAVY PENALTIES—ARTFUL DODGE TO AVOID THE LAW.

> I never in my life
> Did hear a challenge urg'd more modestly.
> SHAKESPEARE.

GEORGE RAYMOND, in his memoirs of Elliston, has recorded an adventure in which I played a considerable part; the facts of which I communicated to him. My friend, however, —for a kinder friend never existed—has embroidered the tale so much that, however amusing he has made it, I must repeat it as it really happened,

The 2nd of May, 18—, was fixed for the royal visit to the theatre, and the monarch of Drury Lane was prepared to give a fraternal welcome to George the Fourth. The King had held a drawing-room at Buckingham Palace on the morning of the day, and a few untoward events, added to the fatigue consequent on the ceremony, found His Majesty not in the most serene temper of mind on his return to Carlton House. But "the best-bred gentleman in the land" was not likely to betray any unseemly feelings of this description to those around him, and the coarse behaviour of the London mob which had followed the royal cortége from the Palace to Pall Mall a few hours before, seemed now altogether to have passed from the memory of the Sovereign. By the King's desire, however, I, as the captain of the escort, was strictly enjoined to ride as close to the carriage-window as possible, never for a moment to leave it. An arrangement wisely preconcerted; for on the morning, as the august party were entering the courtyard, a missile was projected at the King's person, which struck me a pretty palpable hit; the entrance, too, was so narrow that, had it not been for my jack-boot, which was torn to pieces, my leg must have been broken.

So fearful were the authorities that the King would be molested in the Strand that, just before leaving Carlton House for Drury Lane, I was told we were to take a circuitous route by St. Martin's Church and Long Acre.

The doors of the theatre had been beset from an early hour in the afternoon; for the King's visit, on this occasion, appeared to excite more than an ordinary sensation. The rush into the theatre was tremendous. Considerable uproar, from various parts of the house, ensued on disputed seats and packed benches, which, as the King entered the box, increased to such a degree that His Majesty felt impressed with the idea it was directed towards his own person. The Vice-Chamberlain, Lord Graham, in the absence of the Lord Chamberlain, at once perceived the King's feeling, and hastened to address the manager, who was in the waiting-room at the back of the box, that the uproar might be appeased by explanation.

"Mr. Elliston," said his lordship, "this is disgraceful. Why is the theatre so inconsiderately overcrowded? You should have prevented this excess, sir. The King is, naturally, highly vexed, and will never again come to Drury Lane."

This speech, addressed as it was with considerable acrimony to Elliston, surrounded by those attached to the Court, very sensibly nettled him. He replied with equal warmth, but ten times greater dignity,

"My friend will wait upon your lordship;" bowed, and retired to his room.

Quiet having been restored both in the royal box and in the house, I was resting in the ante-room, rather fatigued with my day's work and excitement, when a message was brought to me from Mr. Elliston, requesting that I would at once join him in his private room.

This private room, the temple of Mars, Bacchus, Apollo, and the Cytherean Queen, exhibited, at the moment of my entrance, striking symbols of the various deities, which rendered the room a complete Partheon. I, the captain of the guard *en cuirasse*; Elliston in court-dress, with his sword by his side, a fair and beautiful *artiste*, who retired as I was ushered in; full bottles and empty bottles—the long-necked champagne, bearing Madame Cliquot's name, and the rush-covered curaçoa; plays, playbills, newspapers, tippets, and articles not now heard of, fans and handkerchiefs " of the smallest spider's web," formed a dulcet confusion of effects tending far more at the moment to "puzzle the will" than to offer a calm occasion for the consideration of a most pregnant question.

Elliston, having filled my glass and his own, entered grandiloquently into the nature of his grievance; but I soon perceived that, though the Vice-Chamberlain might have wounded the dignity of the manager, Madame Cliquot's champagne had evidently disordered his wits. I therefore suggested to him that, as a deputy had affronted him, a deputy should reply to it.

"You are right, my lord; my stage-manager shall take up the question in its present shape. I shall not condescend to meet anyone but the Lord-Chamberlain himself. My lord, another glass?—champagne or madeira?"

"Madeira, if you please."

Here Elliston rang the bell, and, on an attendant entering, exclaimed,

"Draw a bottle of Don Pedro's madeira. We will drink, if you please, to the British Army."

"By all means," I replied, "and, let us add, the fair owner of this ivory fan."

On this piece of gallantry, the conversation took a turn so abrupt and so completely of a contrary nature to the great question at issue that I should only interrupt my main narrative by repeating it.

The curtain had fallen on the night's entertainment, the King had returned to Carlton House, had thanked me most graciously for my attention to his commands, the escort had reached the Horse Guards, and, it being now one o'clock of the following morning, I had doffed my leather pantaloons and huge jackboots, preparing to repose myself, when a sharp knock was heard at my door.

"Who's there?" I asked.

"The corporal of the guard," was the reply.

Throwing a dressing-gown over me, I exclaimed,

"Come in."

"One of His Majesty's Lords-in-waiting, I believe, my lord, on urgent business."

"What can it mean?" I exclaimed.

"I know not, my lord; but he said it was on business—'vital,' I think, was the word. The gentleman has been at Court to-day, and is now in the sitting-room."

To the sitting-room I immediately proceeded, where, to my great surprise, I beheld, seated in an arm-chair, no less a personage than the monarch of Drury Lane, King Robert William Elliston, in the same Court gear in which he had an hour or two before attended the monarch of Great Britain.

"I have taken the liberty," observed the new-comer, in a manner even more impressive than his usual delivery, " of ordering a weak glass of brandy and water from the canteen."

Here the manager paused to sip his mixture.

"My lord, we must go out this very morning—I am steady to my purpose," he added, actually reeling in his chair.

I now perceived that a confused recollection of Lord Graham's affront, with a total forgetfulness of the advice he had promised to obey, had brought Elliston from the theatre to the Horse Guards, there to renew his grievance and pass the remainder of the night. My brains were then puzzled how best to get rid of my unexpected guest. I now again pursued the same policy I had taken in the manager's room—namely, representing that it was utterly impossible for him to go out with any deputy; and that, if he did, so far from his honour being vindicated, it would be more deeply involved.

To this Elliston listened as to a perfectly new proposition, and fixing his eyes steadily upon me, during a very lengthened pause, at last said,

"But, my lord, there is one question yet."

"Name it, by all means."

"Might I suggest one more tumbler of brandy and water?"

I now began to take up a policy of my own, and, considering that under the influence of this "one more tumbler," my guest might be less able to offer opposition to my wish of getting rid of him, I gave assent for a replenish of the glass, which was promptly supplied.

Here Elliston drained his tumbler, and rising, not without considerable difficulty, paced the apartment after the manner of one trying thin ice.

"Can I assist you, Elliston?" I asked, offering him his cocked hat, and disentangling his sword from his silken legs.

"By no means; I must be going," drawing out his watch and looking at the reverse side of it.

I then took the manager by the arm, placed the cocked hat upon his head, led him through the passage and down the steps to the street, where a hackney coach was still in waiting.

After some difficulty, and with the aid of the

driver, we got him safely into the vehicle.

"I hope to see you to-morrow, my lord," he exclaimed.

"Certainly," I responded.

I now gave the coachman particular instructions respecting the safe conduct of my friend to his house in Stratford Place, when the man said,

"I'm his honour's own body coachman; have drove his honour for these seven years. All right."

Being now satisfied that Elliston was in the hands of a trustworthy man, I withdrew once more to my own apartment and soon fell asleep, the events of the previous evening flitting before me in my dreams.

In the course of the morning, the following letter reached Mr. Elliston:—

"Wednesday, Grosvenor Square.

"Sir,

"I regret to have heard that you felt hurt at some expression I used towards you the other evening. As this was far from my intention, my only object being to induce you to take some means which would remedy the disorder in the pit, and the unpleasant situation in which persons were in that part of the theatre, as well as the annoyance which it was to His Majesty and the rest of the audience, I feel sorry that you should have misconceived me so as to suppose I would intentionally have said anything disagreeable to you.

"I remain, sir, your obedient
"GRAHAM."

Elliston's reply was as follows:—

"MY LORD,

"I am perfectly satisfied you expressed yourself unguardedly; but it has been observed by one of our best writers that 'an affront handsomely acknowledged becomes an obligation,' and I assure you I fully concur with the spirit of that sentiment. Allow me to add, my lord, that, from my earliest years, I have been bred with the most ardent feelings of respect and duty to my king, and that I have been favoured with so many marks of royal patronage that I should be greatly disturbed could I for an instant neglect the remotest point of attention under any command with which His Majesty might be pleased to honour me. Permit me then to flatter myself with the hope that you may see, in my future endeavours, some cause that may justify the very kind manner in which, my lord, you have so amply healed my wounded feelings. I beg leave to subscribe myself

"Your lordship's most obedient servant,

"R. W. Elliston.

"The most noble The Marquis of Graham."

The laws against what were termed the minor theatres were very stringent, as will be seen by the following actions.

In February, 1835, the Middlesex magistrates having refused to grant a licence to the new Strand Theatre, in defiance of which performances took place, the Lord-Chamberlain, feeling that the offence was committed within the jurisdiction of his office, conceived that he was bound to prosecute, in order that the magistrates might decide whether or not the defendants were justified in assuming the power of dispensing with the laws. In consequence of the above, informations, preferred at the instance of the Earl of Jersey (Lord-Chamberlain) against certain performers of the Strand Theatre for playing for hire without being licensed, were brought forward before Sir Frederick Roe and Mr. Minshank, Mr. Adolphus appearing for the prosecution, and Messrs. Phillips, Clarkson, and Bodkin for the defence.

The first information heard was against William Mitchell, and charged him with having, on the 5th of January, without having obtained a licence from the Lord Chamberlain, performed the part of Fixture at a place called the New Strand Theatre, in a farce, or opera, entitled "A Rowland for an Oliver," contrary to law.

The defendant pleaded not guilty. Mr. Adolphus, after stating the case, thus referred to the evasion the proprietors had resorted to:

"If a person purchased a ticket of admission to the Victoria Theatre, it would entitle such person to a seat in the Strand Theatre. But, even if the public were admitted free to the theatre, the defendants would still be liable to be fined, under another clause in the statute, for selling wines and spirituous liquors on the premises without being licensed."

The learned counsel then called Rodimer, clerk to Mr. Hitchcock, the solicitor for the prosecution, who proved that, on the night of the 5th of January, he went to the Strand Theatre, and purchased a ticket for the Victoria Theatre for two shillings. He observed to a person whom he saw at the door, " This purports to be a ticket for the Victoria Theatre too." To which the person whom he addressed replied, " You can make your selection." He then left the ticket with the person who stood at the door, and passed into the house.

The witness here produced a bill of the entertainments on the nights in question, which he bought in the house. The defendant, Mr. Mitchell, played the part of Fixture in " A Rowland for an Oliver," and Mrs. Waylett performed the character of Maria Darlington. Mrs. Nisbett

MINOR THEATRES.

also performed on the same evening. The witness added that between the performances he went to a small saloon in the theatre, where refreshments were sold, and called for a glass of sherry, for which he paid sixpence.

Henry Nisbett, clerk to Mr. Pritchard, a solicitor in Lincoln's Inn Fields, proved that he went to the Strand Theatre on the same night, and paid four shillings for a ticket for the Victoria, on producing which he was admitted.

The witness Rodimer was then recalled to prove that he searched the records of the Patent Office for the last one hundred years, and found no patent for the Strand Theatre.

Mr. Charles Stewart Addison, from the Lord-Chamberlain's Office, also proved that no licence to allow dramatic performances at the Strand Theatre had been granted by the Lord-Chamberlain.

Sir Frederick Roe, after consulting with Mr. Minshull, said that they were both of opinion that the evidence produced fully bore out the allegations contained in the information, and the defendant must therefore be convicted in the penalty of fifty pounds.

Mr. Forester, another performer at the same theatre, was then charged " with having, on the 5th of January last, performed the part of Alfred Highflyer, in the farce of 'A Rowland for an Oliver,' and in another piece." He was convicted on each information in the penalty of fifty pounds. Rather hard upon a man earning probably five or six pounds a week.

CHAPTER II.

A STROLLING COMPANY—MAIDENHEAD—THEATRICALS IN A BARN—WORCESTER RACES—AN ARCHÆOLOGIST PUZZLED—THE BATTLE OF WORCESTER—WINDSOR THEATRE—A PRACTICAL JOKE.

> Behind the footlights hangs the rusty baize,
> A trifle shabby.
> . . . .
> The stage, methinks, perhaps is none too wide,
> And hardly fit for royal Richard's stride,
> Or Falstaff's bulk, or Denmark's youthful pride.
> . . . .
> A single fiddle is the overture.
> BRET HARTE.

IN by-gone days, when railways were not even in prospective existence, and the transit to London was not as easily managed as it is at the present time, almost every country town had its theatre and its regular company, occasionally illumined by some bright "star" from the metropolis. Generally speaking the manager had a circuit, and, by employing his company all the year round, it was usually an efficient one.

Bath, Bristol, and York fostered early talent; in fact, the above theatres were a sort of nursery, from whence, after a sound education and much practice, the tyro made his appearance before a London audience. If he failed, which was occasionally the case, he went (as it were) back to school again to finish his studies. Whenever an actor or actress acquired a provincial fame, some experienced dramatic manager or stage-manager was dispatched into the country with a discretionary power of engaging the aspirant for one of the two winter theatres, Covent Garden or Drury Lane.

Seldom, if ever, did the above err in their judgment, and, through that judgment, many a clever provincial performer was doomed no longer "to waste" his, or her, "sweetness on the desert air" of a country town. Occasionally, too, on the visit of some London "star," talent that had hitherto been hid "under a bushel" was discovered, and this "flower," hitherto "born to blush unseen," except by a provincial or rural audience, was transplanted to the more genial atmosphere of Covent Garden or the rival house.

In addition to the Metropolitan and the regular country theatres there was a third class, which, Thespian-like, travelled about the country from town to town, displaying their histrionic talents in some large room, at an inn, or in some capacious barn.

While on the subject of strolling players, I am reminded of an "artful dodge," practised many years ago by the manager of one of the above companies who visited Maidenhead during the time my troop was quartered in that town. Understanding that a performance was to take place, a brother officer and myself decided upon dining early at the then celebrated "Sun Hotel," and proceeding to the theatre, or rather to the barn—which had been tastefully fitted up as a Thespian temple. A huge poster at the entrance informed us that a new melodramatic spectacle, entitled " Ivan, the Muscovite, or The Fatal Snowstorm," with a new comic pantomime, called " Old Mother Hubbard, or Harlequin in the Cupboard," would be acted, supported by the whole strength of the company. At the entrance sat the manager's wife, to whom we addressed ourselves, tendering money for two box-seats.

"We do not take money," responded the lady. "My daughters and some friends are about to appear as amateurs, and will be highly flattered if you will honour them with your presence. You can have two front seats, and perhaps you will not object to purchase two boxes of tooth-powder?"

"Certainly not," we responded; and, paying four shillings for the two boxes, we were passed into the theatre.

The performance was really very creditable; the two daughters of the manager showing great histrionic talent. On opening the boxes we found they contained nothing but soot, which, I have no doubt, would have been as good for cleaning the teeth as any rose or other perfumed dentrifice. Many years afterwards, when dining with the late Edmund Byng in Charles Street, I met one of the daughters of the Maidenhead manager. From the strolling company she had been transferred to the regular boards, where she made a brilliant sensation as an actress, and had become the wife of an independent gentleman. I reminded her of the part of Alexina, which she had performed in "Ivan, the Muscovite," at Maidenhead, adding that the prophecy I had then made that she would become a first-rate *artiste* had been realized.

Another adventure occurred to me at Pitchcroft, where the Worcester Races are held. Not caring for races, I persuaded my host, the late Honourable T. Coventry, and some friends who were on a visit to him at his hospitable residence, Severn Stoke, to patronize a theatre, which was temporarily erected.

The play was entitled " Wallenstein, or The Recluse," to be followed by the comic pantomime of "Jack the Giant Killer, or the Cruel Ogre." After paying the large amount of sixpence each for our admission, we were shown to the front row of seats. The band, consisting of a squeaking fiddle, a spasmodic clarionet, and a cracked drum, played an overture, in which "Home, Sweet Home," was the principal feature, a not inappropriate one, as regarded the heroine, for we soon discovered that "Wallenstein" was founded on Kotzebue's "Stranger."

There seemed to be a tacit understanding between the company to drop their H's, or to place them before the third vowel, where they were not wanted. Mrs. 'Aller (as she was called) proved to be the manager's wife, apparently a most useful one, for she took the money at the doors, played the leading parts in tragedy and comedy, and appeared as the Good Fairy of the Silver Lake in the pantomime.

A specimen of the dialogue of "Wallenstein" will be sufficient. When Mrs. Haller inquired of the Countess "whether she had ever heard of the Countess Wallenstein," instead of giving the correct reply, "I have heard of such a wretch at a neighbouring Court. She left her husband and fled with a villain," the unfortunate actress replied, " I 'ave 'eard of such a wretch in a neighbouring court, who left 'er 'usband, and ran off with a villain."

The pantomime was exceedingly funny, inasmuch as the clown, who had acted Peter in the first piece, indulged in the usual stereotyped jocosities of the clown of a travelling circus— " Here we are again !" " Please, sir, he said as I said nothing to nobody !" " I was at the Battle of Watergruel !" Pantaloon—" You mean Waterloo." " Yes; and I cut off a Frenchman's legs !" " Legs ! Why didn't you cut off his head ?" " Because that was already cut off."

The Harlequin was a little too stout for the spangled hero, the Columbine danced with more vigour than grace, the good fairy glittered in spangles from head to foot, while the " lean and slippered Pantaloon " was represented to the life by a worn-out, broken-down, lame old man. Anxious to record what I had seen and heard, I took out my pocket-book to make a few notes. At the conclusion of the performance the manager's wife addressed me as I was going out, and eagerly inquired whether I was connected with the press, as she had observed I had been taking notes. I answered that, although not actually belonging to the "fourth estate" I was a constant contributor to several journals.

"May I hope then," she said, with a most bewitching smile, "that you will condescend to notice hour 'umble hendeavours to please with k*iii*ndness?"

"Nothing would give me greater pleasure," I replied, "but I have no influence with the local newspapers, and I fear the London ones are too much filled with political, home, and foreign news to find space for a provincial theatrical notice."

Nothing more occurred, but in the following October I happened to be in Nottingham, where a detachment of the 4th Hussars were then quartered. Knowing some of the officers, they kindly allowed me to join their mess at the hotel. It was the time of the annual goose fair, and, strolling one afternoon through the marketplace, I noticed the same travelling theatre that I had attended at Worcester. As I passed the door I observed the manager's wife again at her post. She seemed to recognize me, so, approaching her, I expressed a hope that she was doing good business at Nottingham.

"Pretty good," she replied. "Hi 'ope you will 'onour the performance with your presence. We begin punctually at seven. ''Amlet' and 'The Hangel in the Hattic.' I will reserve a front seat for you. I was quite hashamed that a gent connected with the press should have paid at the doors, as you did at Worcester. Hallow me to put you on the free list."

I thanked her cordially, but pleaded an engagement

While upon the subject of Pitchcroft, I cannot refrain from telling a good story attached to it. Upon one occasion, when the Archæological Society visited Worcester, some of the members of that erudite body put up at an hotel. After breakfast one morning, an elderly gentleman, with spectacles on his nose and a hammer in his hand, told the waiter he should require some vehicle to convey him to the scene of the celebrated battle.

"It's within five minutes' walk, sir," responded the member of the slip-shod, white-waistcoated fraternity of "coming, sir."

"Five minutes' walk!" rejoined the astonished archæologist. "I was told it was some few miles off."

"No, sir," persevered the other. "You can see it out of the back windows of the hotel."

"Are you quite sure you are right?" continued the visitor. "I mean the scene of the celebrated battle, fought in——"

"Quite right, sir," interrupted the waiter. "The celebrated battle. I fear it is the last we shall ever see in this neighbourhood."

"Fear!" replied the other, raising his glasses to his forehead, and looking at the waiter, surprise and anger depicted on his countenance, for he was a peaceful character.

"Ah! those were the real good old times," sighed the speaker, "when our hotel was filled —not a spare bed to be had in the town."

PRACTICAL JOKES. 27

"I had no idea your house was of so ancient a date."

"Ancient date! Yes, my master has just been here ten years, and I came a few days before the battle. I saw it from the grand stand. That was a mill! Two finer fellows than Spring and Langan never entered the ring."

Here the mystery was explained. The battle the waiter alluded to was the celebrated pugilistic encounter between the above, and not the Battle of Worcester.

Practical jokes are at all times to be censured, and doubly so when they are practised before an audience. Happily they have been confined to a few. There is a story recorded—I vouch not for its truth—that a celebrated actor, when representing the Ghost in "Hamlet," on ascending the trap, had his legs, which were hid from the spectators, tickled in a manner that made the spirit of Hamlet's father appear more earthly than one risen from the grave. A laughing ghost, lifting his legs as if he was on a treadmill, must have been a sight " more honoured in the breach than the observance," and must have taxed the powers of the Prince of Denmark to refrain from joining the audience in the laugh this untoward jest had brought about.

I read, too, of that arch-hoaxer, Theodore Hook, playing an unwarrantable practical joke at the Haymarket Theatre. Having the *entrée* into the green-room, he managed one evening, during the run of the " Wood Demon," and the excitement of a Westminster Election, to place himself behind the statue of the Demon of the Wood, and, during a breathless silence, to shout "Sheridan for ever!" in the loudest tones the speaking-trumpet was capable of uttering. The cry of "Sheridan for ever!" was taken up by the occupiers of the gallery, who joined in the cry, " Sheridan for ever!"

Another practical joke was played upon the manager of the Windsor Theatre, during the time I was quartered there. Some officers of the Guards and Blues had arranged to get up an amateur performance, for the benefit of some local charity, in which Armitt—" Dick Armitt," of the Guards, than whom a pleasanter or more honourable man never existed—and myself took a deep interest. We had arranged with the proprietor to hand over the theatre to us for a certain number of evenings for rehearsals previous to the night of performance; had engaged actresses, and had ordered dresses from a London costumier; had secured patrons, and were about to announce that the tragedy of "Douglas" and "The Review, or The Wags of Windsor," would be performed by distinguished amateurs, when, upon going to the theatre to arrange the necessary scenery, we found the door locked, and a notice affixed to it, saying that Mr. —— (I will not give his name) was about to open the theatre for an extra week, during which "Douglas" would be performed, to be followed by a favourite afterpiece. To select the very play we were about to act was adding insult to injury.

As an attempt we made to get the proprietor to fulfil his contract with us failed, inasmuch as by his arrangement with Mr. —— the latter could open the theatre whenever he liked, our performance was postponed *sine die*, and never came off. Some of our *corps dramatique* were so "ryled" at the manager's conduct, whose only object was to get us to engage the females of his company and hire the theatre from him, that they vowed vengeance upon his devoted head. The following was the way in which it was carried out:—

For the first five nights not one of the officers attended the theatre, but on the last evening our *corps dramatique* secured two private boxes, much to the delight of the manager, who did all in his power to conciliate us. The plays selected were "The Poor Gentleman" and the burletta of "Midas." In order to facilitate the scheme about to be perpetrated, in securing the two stage-boxes, the head conspirator suggested that any of the one party wishing to join the other should be permitted to cross the stage. This proposition was cheerfully assented to. In the meantime, preparations were made to carry out this Guy Fawkes plot, and a certain number of detonating balls had been procured, which when trod upon would instantaneously explode. The play went off smoothly, and the curtain rose for "Midas," when

> "Jove in his chair,
> Of the sky Lord Mayor,"

appeared, surrounded by the heathen deities. So long as they kept their stations, nothing occurred, but the moment they moved a regular explosion took place. During the confusion more ammunition was being served through the means of pea-shooters, the assailants firing them from behind the curtains of the private boxes. The dark scene was lowered, and the manager came forward to make an appeal to the public to give up the perpetrators of this most disgraceful outrage, offering a reward to be paid on the conviction of the culprit or culprits. The stage having been swept, the curtain again rose, and Jove, represented by the manager, stood up while the chorus was being sung. No sooner did he take possession of his regal chair than another explosion took place; the pea-shooters had done their work cleverly, and, through their unerring aim, the chair was covered with detonating balls. In due course of time, all was cleared away, but the performers, dreading another "blow up," trod the boards as if they were walking on thin ice.

Certainly "Midas" was never acted under such difficulties. One of the company who acted Apollo was equal to the occasion, for, when singing the verse of the song,

> "What more can Bacchus teach men,
> His roaring boys when drunk,
> Than break the lamps, beat watchmen,
> And stagger home dead drunk?"

he came forward, and, gazing steadily, first at one stage-box, then at the other, extemporised the following lines:—

> "What more can Bacchus teach men,
> His roaring boys when drunk,
> With detonators fright men,
> And put them in a funk?"

Rather coarse, but not devoid of art.

Although the perpetrators of the scheme were strongly suspected, not a word escaped their lips, and no active steps were taken to discover them, more especially as the manager's feelings, which had justly been outraged, were soothed by an offer from the amateur *corps dramatique* to give a bespeak, and get rid of a certain number of tickets. This was accordingly done, and an overflowing house was the result.

CHAPTER III

AN ADVENTURE IN CANADA—TORONTO—A STROLLING COMPANY
—NECESSITY THE MOTHER OF INVENTION—AN INCIDENT AT
BOGNOR—MYSTERIOUS MURDER.

> Like wandering Arabs, shift from place to place
> The strolling tribe,
> .   .   .   .
> And, fawning, cringe for wretched means of life
> To Madam Mayoress or his Worship's wife.
> CHURCHILL.

BEFORE I conclude my remarks upon travelling companies, I may refer to one I met in Upper Canada many years ago. At that period I was on my father's staff at Quebec, and, being anxious to visit the Upper Country, accepted an invitation to pass a few days during the summer with a brother-in-law, the late Sir

Peregrine Maitland, who was stationed at Fort York, near the present populous and thriving town of Toronto. At that time Toronto was a very small place; albeit sites for large squares and streets were being laid out.

One morning I rode over to Toronto, then, if I remember right, called "York," where the first object which struck my attention was a large poster, announcing an extraordinary grand performance by Mr. Hatton and his celebrated company, under the immediate patronage of several persons of distinction. The programme ran as follows:—

This Evening will be performed Home's Tragedy of
DOUGLAS;
OR, THE SHEPHERD BOY OF THE GRAMPIAN HILLS.
The part of Young Norval by
MASTER THEODORE HATTON.
Between the play and the after-piece
Comic Songs and Dances.
To conclude with
THE SPOIL'D CHILD.
Little Pickle ... ... MISS JOSEPHINE HATTON.
For further particulars see small bills.
Vivant Rex et Regina!

In vain I sought for a small bill, but on the following evening, when I attended the performance, I soon discovered the reason. Mr. Hatton's *corps dramatique* was very small and very select; he evidently went upon the principle of "not keeping more cats than were necessary for killing the mice," and contented himself with a family group. The result was that each member had to double, occasionally to treble or quadruple a part. Thus Master Theodore, who was a fair-haired stripling, doubled the part of Anna and Young Norval. As the former, he appeared in a loose tartan gown, and the dialogue between him and Lady Randolph was reduced to two lines, not from the pen of the only Scotch dramatist Home— "Oh! mistress most beloved, deign to confide your sacred sorrow to your Anna's breast," which the unhappy widow of the gallant Douglas did in a long speech. Shortly afterwards Anna appeared kilted as the Shepherd Boy, to deliver that celebrated speech so well known to all schoolboys and aspirants for tragedy, "My name is Norval." Many stories, which if fabulous are amusing, are told of this speech. It is said that, upon one occasion, the youth who acted the part disdained all stops, and rapidly proceeded to say,

"My name is Norval on the Grampian Hills."

"And pray," shouted an occupier of the gallery in the Theatre Royal, Dublin, "what is it in the beautiful city of Ould Ireland?"

Upon another occasion, we hear of an infant prodigy, as he was called, who, upon appearing on the boards, was so nervous that he could not utter a word. Finding this, the actor, who was representing Lord Randolph, came to the rescue of the "dummy" and said,

"This youth's name is Norval; on the Grampian Hills his father fed his flock; a frugal swain, whose constant care was to increase his store, and keep his only son, this youth, at home," &c., &c.

Of Master Hatton's performance of the above character, I will merely say that, when in the last act he falls through the treachery of a foe to the house, his death was hailed with cheers, whether from the high conception he had of the character, or the delight of the audience in not seeing him again, must remain a mystery except in the breasts of those who were present on that occasion.

Mrs. Hatton appeared as Lady Randolph, and danced the Highland Fling in character, which was much more like an Ojibaway dance than the national one, and acted Little Pickles in the farce, in which she sang that beautiful ballad immortalized by Mrs. Jordan, "Since then I'm doomed." Mrs. Hatton might have proved equally successful, but, unfortunately, this lady was like one of the members of the Nightingale Club as referred to in the comic medley of that name.

"The Nightingale Club in the village was held
   At the sign of the 'Cabbage and Shears,'
Where the singers no doubt would have greatly excelled
   But for want both of taste, voice, and ears."

Mrs. Hatton doubled the parts of Glenalvon and The Trembling Coward who forsook his Master, in the tragedy, and acted Pag and another part in the farce. An elderly man, who made himself generally useful as musician, prompter, bill-poster, and actor, represented Lord Randolph, and also appeared in the afterpiece in more than one character.

In the following October, when my father visited Kingstown officially, as Governor-General of Canada, I found that Mr. Hatton, with an increased *corps dramatique*, was acting at the theatre, and, wishing to give him a good turn, persuaded my father to give a bespeak, and to attend the performance. Inspired by this, the Protean manager wrote and spoke a complimentary address. I remember two lines:

"If Richmond then approve, we will not yield,
But pitch our tent e'en here at Bosworth Field."

Another incident connected with the theatre must be recorded. It occurred some years ago, and created the deepest interest. During the last meeting of what the sporting newspapers term "Glorious Goodwood," I passed the week at Bognor. Strolling out one evening, I came to the spot where the circumstance took place, when the whole scene came vividly back to my mind, and for the first time I committed it to paper. It was early in the present century, when I, as a boy, was sent with a tutor to a farm-house at Feltham, near Bognor. One day when we were driving towards Berstead, my tutor's attention was attracted to a placard, upon which appeared, in large letters, "Murder, one hundred pounds' reward." It then stated "that the above sum would be paid to anyone who would give information that would lead to the apprehension of the murderer." From that moment the curiosity of the then small villages of Bognor and Feltham was raised to the greatest extent; that a murder had been committed no one for a moment doubted, for it was proved that a dagger and a piece of cloth, both stained with blood, had been found under the flooring of a dilapidated barn about to be pulled down, and that a paper had been discovered, on which was written, "My wrongs are avenged, my hated rival ceases to live." The magistrates of the neighbouring towns held sundry meetings, the constables were on the alert, and the soldiers received orders to keep a strict watch on all suspicious characters. In those days two squadrons of light cavalry quartered at Chichester were stationed at different villages on the coast to aid the civil officers against the smugglers.

"It is as clear as the sun at midday," said a superannuated guardian of the peace, while enjoying his clay pipe at a small public house in Bognor, now swept away, "that a heinous murder has been committed, and my impression is that Jim Mader and Isaac Hindley had some hand in it; they are *ow*dacious poachers, and vowed vengeance against a comrade who they thought would peach against them."

"Ah, Mr. Gribble" (I give fictitious names so as not to offend any descendants, should they exist), "you're always right," responded a brother constable, "and I know well that those two ruffians were hovering about near the barn where the awful deed was perpetrated."

Such were the sentiments of all in the neighbourhood, high and low, rich and poor, peer and peasant, that is, as regards a murder having been committed, though some were more charitable as to the suspected persons, thinking that, though a man might be a poacher, it did not follow that he added to his guilt by breaking the sixth commandment. Time circled on, and, despite the exertions of the lord-lieutenant of the county, the magistrates, and the constables, no clue to the mystery was afforded.

In the summer of the following year, a company of strolling players came to Bognor in search of a Thespian temple in which to display their dramatic powers. It was their first visit to the town, if such a term could fairly be applied to a small village, and they were at last located in an out-house, near where the Clarence Hotel now stands. The leading tragedian, whose real name was Roberts, but who acted under the *nom de théâtre* of Mr. John Philip Fitzwalter, had prevailed upon a publican to lodge and board him for a fortnight. In those days all actors were, in the eyes of the law, looked upon as "vagrants and vagabonds." Strolling players were, more especially, under a ban, as was illustrated by the common saying, — "Take in the linen from the lines, the players are coming."

Few publicans then, or lodging-house keepers, were ambitious of their custom, but Miles Stavely, of "The Anchor," had, by a promise of a certain number of tickets upon Mr. Fitzwalter's benefit night, consented to take him in during his stay at Bognor. One eventful evening, after a performance which had been honoured by a bespeak of a neighbouring squire, and salaries had been paid, Miles Stavely invited the "eminent tragedian" to take a glass with him in the bar-parlour, an invitation strongly backed up by the publican's niece, who acted as barmaid, and who had been greatly smitten by the personal appearance of Mr. Fitzwalter when he appeared as Manfredi, in a tragedy entitled, "The Brigand Chief, or Italian Revenge." After sundry glasses of punch had been quaffed, the attention of Fitzwalter was attracted to a placard on the wall. His eye caught the words of "The old barn, between Bognor and Feltham;" the identical barn in which he had the year before, to use his own expression, "coal'd it" and "brought the house down."

"Why! What is this?" he exclaimed, in a pompous tone, as he rose from his chair, and approached the printed notice. "'One hundred pounds' reward will be paid to anyone giving information that may lead to the apprehension of the murderer of a person unknown, on or about the 10th day of July, 18— The weapon with which the deed is supposed to have been perpetrated may be seen at the Town Hall, Chichester, on application to the Clerk of the Peace. Twenty-five pounds will be paid to any person who may throw a light upon the mystery that now exists.'"

Fitzwalter started back, exclaiming with Hamlet:

"There are more things in heaven and earth, Horatio,
Than are dreamt of in your philosophy."

"How far is it to Chichester?" he hurriedly asked.

"About seven miles," was the reply. "And if you are anxious to go there," continued the landlord, "as you have paid me so handsomely for your board and lodging, you may have a

A COURT OF JUSTICE. 45

seat in my dog-cart, which I shall drive over in early to-morrow morning."

"Thanks, generous friend," replied Mr. Fitzwalter. "Gladly do I accept your offer."

At an early hour next morning the two started for Chichester; Fitzwalter keeping to himself the secret. Upon reaching that city he immediately proceeded to the Town Hall, where the magistrates were sitting. Certainly his appearance did not command much respect. His dress, to adopt a common phrase, was "awfully seedy," and not improved by the dust he had met with on the road. With some difficulty he made his way through the crowd of lookers-on down to the barrier which separated them from the bench.

"Stand back," exclaimed a constable.

"I have a statement to make to the magistrates," said Fitzwalter.

"Silence in the Court," shouted the usher.

"Are you about to apply for a warrant or a summons?" inquired the clerk.

"Neither," responded the actor. "My business is with the magistrates."

"Remove that man, constable," said one of the "unpaid," hearing the discussion.

Fortunately, at that moment, the squire who had patronized the performance on the previous evening entered the hall, and took his seat upon the bench.

"What do you require, Mr. Fitzwalter?" he mildly asked, thinking it was probably a request to give a temporary licence to the strolling company.

"I thank you, sir. I appear before this worthy bench to give a clue to the mystery that has so long puzzled the wisest of heads."— There was a dead silence.—"In the month of July last year, I was acting my favourite character of the Pirate Chief, in the old barn near Bognor, and, in the hurry of our departure, I left behind me a dagger, apparently stained with blood, also a paper, on which the following lines were written, 'My wrongs are avenged; my hated rival ceases to live!'"

"That's all very well," remarked the testy man in brief authority, who had ordered the intruder to be removed, "but you, or some of your strolling friends, may have inspected the dagger and paper."

"If you require further proof, 'consummation strong as Holy Writ,' I will furnish it. The dagger was originally a midshipman's dirk when it came into my possession, and I used it as a 'property.'"

"A what?" again interrupted the surly magistrate.

"A property, your worship; a theatrical phrase, used to represent the different articles required in a drama. On becoming possessor of it I had the handle, which is an ivory one, covered with cord, with the double view of preserving it and rendering it more fit to be used by me as the Pirate Blackbeard."

"And may I ask you how this dagger, or dirk, as you call it, came into your hands?" continued the magistrate.

"My father, Maurice Roberts, was a midshipman on board Admiral Rodney's ship, when he fought, near Cape St. Vincent, the Spanish Admiral Don Langara, whom he defeated, and made prisoner, capturing six of the ships, one of which blew up. In this action my father was killed, and his gallant captain forwarded my uncle the dirk, which was to be kept for me until I entered my fifteenth year, with a hope that I should follow my lamented parent's profession. I was, in due course of time, entered as a clerk in my uncle's office. 'A roving disposition, good my lord,' led me to abandon law for the stage, when I took the name of John Philip Fitzwalter, my real appellation being simple John Roberts."

"A very pretty story; probably founded on some stage play," said the still sceptical magistrate, when the warm-hearted squire came to Fitzwalter's assistance.

"Is there any mark under the cord, with which you say you enclosed the handle, that can identify the dirk as having belonged to your father?"

"There is, sir," John Roberts replied. "The initials of my father, M.R., are engraved on the ivory handle."

The dagger was sent for, the cord removed. When the *denouement* was brought about there was a grand sensation in the Court. Fitzwalter received the reward, five and twenty pounds, with which sum he became the manager of a country theatre. Fortune favoured him; in time he extended his theatrical business to a well-paying circuit, married the publican's niece, and, for all I know to the contrary, received the usual benediction, "Bless you, my children."

CHAPTER IV.

DRAMATIC AUTHORS—THOMAS MORTON—GEORGE COLMAN—POOLE—AN EPISODE—" THE GALLEY SLAVES "—R. B. PEAKE—A LOVE CHASE—THE HUNDRED POUND NOTE—REVEREND DR. CROLY—" PRIDE SHALL HAVE A FALL "—KENNEY—" RAISING THE WIND "—A LOST VOICE—PLANCHÉ—SHERIDAN KNOWLES—THEODORE HOOK—TEKELI IN A TUB.

The whole theatre resounds with the praises of the great dramatists, and the wonderful art and order of the corporation.

BURNET.

I HAVE had the good fortune, during a very long career, to be acquainted with many dramatic authors, and have passed many agreeable hours in their society. Thomas Morton, the author of some of our most popular comedies, and father of Maddison Morton, who has evidently inherited much of his parent's genius, was a most remarkably kind-hearted and genial character, and I constantly met him at Mr. Harris's, when the latter was manager of Covent Garden Theatre. Thomas Morton's principal contributions to the stage were " Speed the Plough," "Cure for the Heart-Ache," "School of Reform," "A Roland for an Oliver."

George Colman I knew intimately, and often visited him when living in Melina Place, within the rules of the King's Bench. He was the Yorick of his days, whose flashes of merriment were wont to set the table in a roar. Byron thus describes his social qualities:—" If I had to choose, and could not have both at a time, I should say, 'Let me begin the evening with Sheridan, and finish it with Colman—Sheridan for dinner, and Colman for supper—Sheridan for claret or port, but Colman for everything. Sheridan was a grenadier company of Life Guards, but Colman a whole regiment—of light infantry, to be sure, but still a regiment." He has left a literary and dramatic legacy behind him in plays, farces, poetry, and song. Among the best may be mentioned "The Heir-at-law," "John Bull," "The Poor Gentleman." He also produced "The Mountaineers," and "Inkle and Yarico." Colman died in October, 1836.

Poole, the author of "Paul Pry," "Intrigue," "Who's Who?" and "Scorpion and Co.," &c., &c., possessed a large amount of quiet humour, little deserving the angry reply of Elliston after some theatrical squabble, when the pompous monarch of Drury Lane addressed him as follows:—"I have heard of a puddle in a storm and a *pool* in a passion—I treat both with contempt." Poole, if I remember right, was the first writer who parodied Shakespeare; his "Hamlete Travesti" is humorous enough to burst the belt of an anchorite with laughter; and here I hope to be pardoned for an act of egotism, for which I plead guilty, and throw myself upon the mercy of my readers.

Some forty years ago, more or less, a drama was brought out at one of the winter theatres, entitled, "The Galley Slaves," when it occurred to me that a parody upon it might prove successful. I therefore at once set to work, and shortly presented the piece, under the title of "The Gallows Slaves," to Mr. Egerton, at that time manager of the Olympic Theatre. It was accepted, and put into rehearsal under the superintendence of that gentleman, for I wished to follow at a very great distance the example of "The Great Unknown," and not appear as the author. At that period the treadmill was just introduced, and it occurred to me that a scene introducing "The Gallows Slaves," and others upon it, singing a parody on "We are all nodding, nid, nid, nodding," altering the words to "We are all treading, tread, tread, treading," would be effective. The whole was written in doggerel verse, the songs adapted to the popular melodies of that day. "Upon their own merits modest men are dumb," so says the erudite Dr. Pangloss. I will therefore only say that the piece ran through the season, and was printed in Little Queen Street, Chancery Lane. I had a copy, which has long since been "absent without leave."

The above, and a musical farce, entitled, "Incog., or Tied by the Leg," were my only productions. "Incog." was acted with a tolerable amount of success at the Hawker's Street Theatre, Dublin, but, though approved of by Mr. Arnold, it only ran three nights at the Lyceum Theatre, then under his management. It was produced during my temporary absence in Ireland, with no one to attend or make suggestions during the rehearsals. Whether it met with the fate it deserved, it is not for me to say; all I know is that on the third night the piece was *condemned* (I use a mild phrase); it was afterwards *burnt* when the Lyceum Theatre was destroyed by fire.

Richard Brinsley Peake, treasurer for many years at the English Opera House, now Lyceum Theatre, and by his name probably a godson of the great Brinsley Sheridan, seemed to have partaken in a considerable degree of his godfather's wit, for a more witty man never existed. He was equal to Theodore Hook in punning, and I am surprised that no collection of his "sayings" has been recorded. Many, however, of his best puns, of which I remember a few, were upon local subjects, and, therefore, lose much of their point when repeated, after the subject has been forgotten. Moreover, there is a way of saying a smart thing which Peake possessed to an eminent degree. A pun, like an omelette, a pancake, or a fondu, should be furnished hissing hot from the intellectual furnace; it becomes cold and heavy after a time. Many of our best farces were written by Peake, notably "Amateurs and Actors," in which Wrench as Wing, Wilkinson as Geoffery Muffincap, Harley as O. P. Bustle, Pearman as David Dulcet, Esq., and Miss Pincett as Mrs. Mary Goneril, made a great sensation.

I claim the merit of having given Peake a suggestion for a farce, which he availed himself of. It was founded upon an occurrence in real life which took place at one of our large manufacturing towns when Miss M. Tree, afterwards Mrs. Bradshaw, was fulfilling a "starring" engagement. Mr. Bradshaw, a London exquisite, possessed of a large fortune, became enamoured of the lovely Maria, and followed her into the country. Every evening he took up his station in a private box near the stage, and, I have no doubt, heaped floral bouquets upon the object of his admiration. At the termination of Miss M. Tree's engagement, her devoted admirer, who was staying at the leading hotel under the assumed name of Brown, called for his bill, and in payment gave a cheque signed in his real name. His thoughts were probably more on the inimitable Clair than on business, or he never would have been guilty of such an inadvertence. The waiter looked at the cheque, opened his eyes, stared at the guest, removed some silver forks from the sideboard, and withdrew. As Bradshaw was leaving the hotel to take a stroll previous to the time when his travelling-carriage and pair had been ordered, he could not help remarking that the landlady at the bar looked rather suspiciously at him, and the porter, at a most respectful distance, was following his steps. In the meantime, the landlord had rushed off to the bank, where he was informed that a cheque of Mr. James Bradshaw's, if genuine, would be honoured to any amount; the only question was whether the cheque was genuine or spurious. While deliberating what was to be done, one of the partners made his appearance, and said that he would at once solve the mystery, as he had met Mr. Bradshaw in London, and could easily recognise his features. As they were leaving the bank to proceed to the hotel, the real "Simon Pure" came in, for a sudden thought had reminded him that the name he had assumed at the hotel was not the one in which he had drawn the cheque.

"Mr. Bradshaw, I am happy to see you," said the banker. "Do you wish notes or gold for the cheque which has just been presented?"

"A fifty pound note, the rest in gold."

The landlord, who had listened attentively to the above conversation, smiled placidly, handed the cheque to the cashier, received the amount, and, bowing respectfully to Mr. Bradshaw, left the bank.

"We've nearly lost a good customer," exclaimed his better half, as he explained the affair, "and all along with your vile suspicions."

"But, my dear——"

"Don't dear me; I always looked upon our guest as quite the gentleman."

This matrimonial squabble was put an end to by the entrance of the waiter, who said "the gent in No. 3 was waiting for a receipt and his change."

The carriage was shortly afterwards announced, and Mr. Bradshaw, *alias* Brown, stepped into it, and was driven off at the rate of ten miles an hour on his way back to London.

Hearing at White's Club of the above adventure, I accidentally mentioned it to Peake, who took advantage of the suggestion, dramatised it, and, under the title of "The Hundred Pound Note," brought it out at the Lyceum Theatre.

During the rehearsal of "Pride shall have a Fall," by the Reverend Dr. Croly, I got acquainted with the author, who, albeit a good divine, and a clever dramatist, required a few hints as to military life, with which I was only too happy to furnish him. Although the scene was laid at Palermo, I felt that officers in all civilised countries generally follow the same pursuits—namely, flirting, playing at billiards, eating, and drinking. The play was admirably well performed, W. Farren, C. Kemble, Yates, Jones, Egerton, Blanchard, Abbott, Mrs. Davenport taking the leading parts in the comedy, and the best musical talent of the day undertaking the vocal parts. The only drawback, to my mind, was that singing was introduced. In the first place, few vocalists can act comedy well; secondly, a bravura in the midst of an interesting scene is sadly out of place. What should we think if Lady Teazle, after her quarrel with Sir Peter, were to favour the company with a song; Miss Hardcastle, in "She Stoops to Conquer," to warble a ditty when disguised as a chambermaid; or Julia, in "The Rivals," to gratify the jealous Falkland by singing a ballad? Of course, if the above innovations were sanctioned, an appropriate song for Lady Teazle would be:

"An old man would be wooing
 A damsel fair and young,
But she whom he was suing
 For ever laughed and sung.
An old man, an old man will never do for me,
For May and December will never, will never agree."

Julia might console Falkland by singing :

"But should my lover
 Ever discover
Jealousy, folly, I'll answer him so :
 Dearest, believe me,
 I'll ne'er deceive ye,
You have my heart, others have but the show."

To return to "Pride shall have a Fall." The epilogue spoken by Yates as Cornet Count Carmine, in which he introduced his imitations of London actors, proved a wonderful success. It ran as follows :—

(He hurries on.)

"Ladies and gentlemen,—Quite out of breath—
 Ten thousand pardons!—teas'd, star'd, talked to death—
 Found it scarce possible to get away ;—
 Those green-room persons—monstrous deal to say—
 Queens, heroes, ghosts, priests, ploughmen,—to full
   swing,—
 I'll give you some few touches of the thing."

IMITATIONS.

C. Young:

"A comedy! A new-born miracle!
Comes it with airs from heaven or blasts from hell?
Is it a spirit of health or goblin damned?"

Fawcett:

"Pooh! fudge and nonsense! Are the boxes crammed?"

Dowton:

"The pit has had a fainting match and fight;
Of course, you'll have it acted every night?"

Fawcett:

"Boy, print to-morrow's bills:—*No standing-room*,
And *Not an order* for a year to come."

Mrs. Davenport as Mrs. Malaprop:

"Has it no scandal in it? no lord's jobation?
No lady-bird? no crim-concatenation?"

W. Farren as Sir Fretful Plagiary:

"See act the fifth. That 'elevates'—surprises."

Blanchard:

"I think it falls."

W. Farren:

"You mean, sir, rises—rises."

Blanchard :

" 'Tis passable.   His next, perhaps, will mend."

W. Farren :

" 'Tis *possible!* (a d—d good-natur'd friend)."

C. Mathews :

" No scalping's in't, no squaws.   My friends the Yankees
For ten such plays, *I guess,* won't give ten thankees."

Connor :

" Sir, that's a plain affront !   I like the play ;
Such nights as these, sir, aren't seen every day."

Terry :

" Such nights !   I tell you that those things won't *tell.*
Why didn't he dramatise ' St. Ronan's Well ',?
Write *wholesale* from my friend Sir Walter's page ?"

Munden :

" The *Well!*   Ay !   Read water on the stage !
Why, Drury !   Zounds !   He'd drown your *Cataract.*'

Elliston :

" He drown my—I'll but state one stubborn fact :
Ladies and gentlemen,—These fifty years—
Lend me your ears (such of you as have ears)—
That piece *shall* run !   I always speak my mind ;
The *Water* is the way to *raise* the *Wind.*
And, since I've *wet,* I'll *dry* the British nation
My benefit night—the *General Conflagration.*"

Farley:

"D'ye think the author has a knack for rhyme?
I'll make him *Laureate* of the pantomime."

Macready as Virginius:

"His cast is good. The man must have no fear,
Were but 'my daughter, my Virginia,' there."

Raynor:

"I luve Victoria!* She's my heart, my loife;
Tuch her who dare, she'd make a pretty woife."

Incledon as Macbeth:

"May my mare slip her shoulder, but I'll take
The young un."

Braham:

"Gentlemen, for Shakespeare's sake,
Leave us our Nightingales—we want them all;
Falstaff himself, without them *now*, must fall."

Kemble:

"Shakespeare to music! Every inch a king!
Richard is *hoarse*, I'll choke before *I'll sing*."

Cornet Count Carmine:

"At length, escaped—myself again—alone—
I supplicate at Beauty's native throne.

---

* The "Victoria" here referred to was a character in the drama.

By the high splendours of our ancient days;
By those we've seen, and wept to see—decay;
By our, by *mankind's* SHERIDAN, whose tomb
Is scarcely closed!
     But no,—no thoughts of gloom!
Again comes COMEDY! So long untried!
Give her your smiles!
     The victory's on our side.
Your smiles have won the day! Thanks each and all,
Now, now indeed, '*our* pride shall have no fall'!"

"Pride shall have a Fall" was first acted at Covent Garden Theatre on the 11th of March, 1824. Sheridan died in 1816, so the writer of the epilogue indulged in poetical licence when he talks of his tomb being "scarcely closed."

I met Kennedy, the author of "Raising the Wind," occasionally; had I known him before the incident I am about to record happened, he would have laughed heartily, especially as it was connected with the above farce, which still retains its popularity on the boards. Many years ago, when serving upon my father's staff at Quebec, theatricals were got up in that garrison, and upon one occasion I acted Jeremy Diddler. In the printed edition of that piece the author says that at the opening scene in the second act, when Diddler is making love to the old maid, Miss Laurelia Durable, and the young, pretty, blooming Kitty, the song of "My beautiful Maid" ought to be introduced; but, as few actors of farce are able to sing, it is universally omitted. Now, albeit I belonged to that class of (I fear I cannot say actors) amateurs who cannot turn a tune, I naturally could not myself introduce the ballad; it however occurred to me that a friend, Mr. Tolfrey, who also took part in our theatricals and was a splendid singer, might be my substitute, which he good-humouredly consented to be.

To carry out the scheme, I had the supper-table placed quite at the back of the stage, and had a slit made in the scene, behind which my "double" was to remain waiting for his "cue" —"A song, a song, Mr. Diddler."

On the evening of the performance the first act went off very well; on the curtain rising for the second, the untoward event took place. My friend, after finishing the song, which was rapturously applauded, ran off to the dressing-room to change his dress; he had acted Mr. Hardcastle in the opening piece, and that costume was not at all suited to keep off the cold of a Canadian winter night. A cry of "encore" was now raised in the gallery, and taken up by many of the audience in the boxes and pit. Thinking my "voice" was still in waiting, the company at the table cried out, "Bravo, Mr. Diddler, pray sing it again." I bowed, and listened, in the hopes of hearing the first notes, but no notes were forthcoming. The clamours increased, for on that day a regiment of the line had arrived from Gibraltar, and the officers of the regiment, never having seen me before, naturally thought that I was a vocalist, and wished to pay just compliment to my musical abilities.

"Where's Mr. Tolfrey?" I asked, *sotto voce*, of the prompter, who happened to be standing at the wing.

"I've sent for him, but he is half undressed," replied the man.

Nothing, then, was left for me but to apologise to the audience; so, leaving my seat at the table, I approached the foot-lights, and addressed them as follows:—

"Ladies and gentlemen,—Nothing can be more gratifying to any performer, whether professional or amateur, than the applause of the public," ("Bravo! bravo!") "and I feel deeply the compliment you have kindly paid me. I have, however, unfortunately lost my voice. Under these circumstances, perhaps you will permit the performance to proceed." ("Bravo! bravo!")

I returned to my seat, and was still acknowledging the "bravos," when, to my surprise, I found my voice had returned; Tolfrey had been summoned. He rushed down (good fellow as he was) in his dressing-gown, and began the song again. Athough a little flustered at this unexpected apparition, I soon recovered my presence of mind, opened my mouth, and carried out the deception.

Poor Planché, who lived to a good old age, was one of my earliest acquaintances; it seems but a few weeks ago that I had a long conversation with him at Mrs. Freake's *tableaux*, when we talked over old times. Planché was one of the kindest-hearted men I ever knew; I never heard him say an ill-natured thing of anyone. He belonged to that class of amiable individuals whom Douglas Jerrold describes as "being ready to hold an umbrella over a duck during a shower of rain!" As a dramatist and a writer on heraldry few could excel him. Well did he merit the praise showered upon his numerous works for the stage and upon costume, and nobly did he fill his heraldic office, graciously granted him by the Sovereign.

Planché first came into theatrical notice by a burlesque, after the fashion of "Tom Thumb" and "Bombastes Furioso," entitled "Amororo, King of Little Britain." It was brought out at Drury Lane, with Harley as the hero; the music was well selected, the popular melodies of the day forming the principal feature. It was just before "Amororo" appeared that I became acquainted with the author, who asked me to attend a rehearsal, which I did.

I at once felt that it would be admirably well suited for amateurs, and would prove a novelty at Quebec, whither I was about to proceed, and where I hoped to get up some garrison theatricals. I was confirmed in this opinion at the first representation, and Planché obligingly promised to send me a prompter's marked copy, should it not be published before my departure. I was quite right in my anticipations; for we acted it twice at Quebec to large and appreciative audiences.

To prove how times are changed, and what rapid strides have been made by the march of improvement, I will remark that, in "Amororo," the King sings a song, pointing out that such and such things are next to impossible. If I recollect aright, His Majesty refers to " steam-boats," " extraordinary cast-iron bridges," etc., and declaring:

"When steam-boats no more on the Thames shall be flowing,
Why then, Molly Quita, I'll love thee no more."

Had the King lived a few years longer he

would have seen how erroneous were his former notions.

Planché's fairy pieces, which were brought out during the period Madame Vestris ruled over the destinies of the Olympic Theatre, contributed not a little to the success of the undertaking, while his more important works have earned for him a name that will never be forgotten so long as there is a taste for genuine dramatic power and pleasing poetry; for his songs lay claim to the title of poetry.

Sheridan Knowles I often met, and was always charmed with his society. He was a warm-hearted Irishman, very agreeable, excellent company, and devoted for many years to the drama, to which he was a most liberal contributor. He was the author of "The Love Chase," "Woman's Wit," "Old Maids," "The Rose of Aragon," "The Secretary," "William Tell," "Alfred the Great," "Love," "The Beggar of Bethnal Green," "John of Procida," "The Maid of Mariendorpt," "Caius Gracchus," and, last not least, "Virginius," in which Macready made so great a sensation.

With Theodore Hook, another successful dramatist, I was on terms of intimate friendship; but, during my acquaintance with him, he had given up writing for the stage, and devoted his talents, which to a certain degree, and in a particular line, were wonderful, to the *John Bull* newspaper, and novel writing.

Byron thus refers to "Tekeli"—

> "Now to the drama turn. Oh! motley sight!
> What precious scenes the wondering eyes invite!
> Puns and a prince within a barrel pent."

In a note to the above the noble bard says: "In the melodrama of 'Tekeli,' a heroic prince is clapt into a barrel on the stage," a new asylum for distressed heroes.

The critics were very severe on "Tekeli," which was pronounced to be "a mere vehicle for scenery and music, which cannot challenge commendation, and scarcely ought to provoke criticism."

Hook was an inveterate punster. I well remember one day remarking to him that there had been a sad fatality among the theatres, and that the Exeter Theatre had been recently burnt to the ground.

"Quite theatrical," he replied ; "enter a fire, exit a theatre" (Exeter Theatre).

CHAPTER V.

DRAMATIC AUTHORS—TOM TAYLOR—THE OLD STAGERS—BUCK-STONE—THE DIBDINS—MARK LEMON—AN ACTOR'S FEAST—BURNAND—BYRON—PALGRAVE SIMPSON—BARHAM LIVIUS—H. R. ADDISON.

An author has the choice of his own thoughts and words, which a translator has not.
DRYDEN.

MY acquaintance with Tom Taylor was brief, but I saw enough of him to be delighted with his conversational powers, his wit, and his readiness to do all in his power to promote the hilarity of those around him. Upon two occasions I was present at the Canterbury cricket week, and a more enjoyable time cannot well be imagined. A match in the morning by the best players of this truly national game, the ground graced by the presence of the loveliest of the gentler sex, military bands enlivening the amusement by their dulcet or impassioned strains, officers of the garrison vying with each other in their attention to their fair friends and guests, luncheon tents with every delicacy of the season—the choicest wines and the most cooling "cups"—through the liberality of the gallant members of the cavalry depot or regiment of the line quartered in the barracks. Then at night the amateur theatricals by the "Old Stagers," a *corps dramatique* unequalled, and whose performances, aided by female professional talent, would do honour to the regular boards. Among this "band of brothers" jealousy does not exist; every member puts his shoulder to the wheel, and does his best to promote the interest of the whole. Never shall I forget Tom Holmes (he will forgive this familiarity, which I trust will reverse the adage and not breed contempt) appearing as a German waiter. The scene, if I remember rightly, was laid at Homburg, and, although he had only to lay the table and wait upon the guests, he rendered the trifling part a most prominent feature, reminding one of the story told of Garrick, who, at an amateur performance, noticed a servant as the only good actor of the lot, and he turned out to be a professional one.

To return to the author of "'Twixt Axe and Crown." During my visit to Canterbury, the amateur *corps dramatique* allowed me to join their party at the "Fountain Hotel." Tom Taylor was manager and epilogue writer. Of the acting, I will merely say that it was faultless; for the Old Stagers are not content, as many amateurs are, to appear on the boards without a sufficient number of rehearsals, but they devote their mornings to going through every scene correctly from the beginning to the end. Hence the success. With them there is no saying, "I'll do it at night," for the acting manager peremptorily insists that all that is to be done at night is to be gone through in the morning.

After the play supper was announced, and

then began the fun of the evening. Songs, jests, and *reparties* were carried on with the greatest hilarity until midnight, when an extemporaneous performance took place under the immediate direction of Tom Taylor. He suggested the idea, gave valuable hints, superintended the dresses of the respective characters—which were improvised out of curtains, table covers, kitchen utensils—and took a prominent part for himself. Then the mirth began fast and furious, but never outstepped its proper bounds. The only regret that I had was that some shorthand writer was not present upon the same evening, to have noted down the performance. Tom Taylor was a very versatile writer; he could grasp history, furnish incidents of the deepest interest, turning from grave to gay, and producing the most humorous farces of the day. His memory will long be enshrined in the hearts of all who had the good fortune to know him during his brilliant career as a critic, a dramatist, a journalist, and social companion.

In addition to Tom Taylor's celebrated historical drama of "'Twixt Axe and Crown," he was the author of the following pieces, all of which proved highly successful: "Still Waters run Deep," "The Vicar of Wakefield," "Plot and Passion," "Helping Hands," "Slave Life," "The King's Rival," "Two Loves and a Life," and of the following farces: "A Blighted Being," "To Parents and Guardians," "Our Clerks;" he was also one of the authors of "Masks and Faces."

John Baldwin Buckstone, with whom I was on terms of intimacy, ranked high as an actor and dramatic writer. He was originally intended for the navy, but, his naval taste being checked, he was articled to a solicitor. Preferring the studying of parts to the copying of legal documents, he quitted the office, and, at the early age of nineteen, made his first appearance on the boards at Wokingham, Bucks, where, owing to the sudden illness of the first comedian of a travelling company, he, at an hour's notice, was called upon to take the part of Gabriel in "The Children in the Wood." His *début* on this occasion was thoroughly successful and gave promise of a splendid future career, which, ere long, was realized. Mr. Buckstone next became a member of a friend's company, who had recently become lessee of the Faversham, Folkestone, and Hastings Theatres.

In 1824 Mr. T. Dibdin resigned the management of the Surrey Theatre, and his successor, Mr. W. Burroughs, engaged the services of Buckstone, who made his first appearance before a metropolitan audience as Peter Smink in "The Armistice." His fame soon spread abroad, and reached the ears of Mr. Perry, at that time manager of the Adelphi Theatre, who enlisted his services, and brought him out as Bobby Trot in "Luke the Labourer." Whilst at the Adelphi Mr. Buckstone found time to write several pieces for the Haymarket Theatre, which eventually led Mr. Morris to engage him.

From the year 1837 up to his death Mr. Buckstone was associated with the Haymarket Theatre as author, actor, manager, and lessee; visiting during that period the United States, and, for a short period, forming one of Madame

Vestris's company at the Lyceum, and one of Mr. Bunn's at Drury Lane.

From his fertile pen have emanated numerous comedies, dramas, and farces; the quality being quite equal to the quantity. Among them may be mentioned "Popping the Question," "Our Mary Anne," "Luke the Labourer," "John Street, Adelphi," "The Wreck Ashore," "Victorine," "The King of the Alps," adapted from the German, "The Rake and the Pupil," "The May Queen," "Henriette the Forsaken," "Isabelle, or Woman's Life," and "The Dream at Sea." His early plays at the Haymarket were "A Husband at Sight," "John Jones," "Uncle John," "Second Thoughts," "Married Life," "Single Life," "A Lesson for Ladies," "Nicholas Flann," "Naval Felicity," "Weak Points," "The Thimble Rig," and "The Irish Lion." He subsequently produced there his three-act comedy, "Leap-year, or the Ladies' Privilege," "An Alarming Sacrifice," and "Good for Nothing."

During Madame Celeste's management of the Adelphi he produced "The Green Bushes" and "The Flowers of the Forest," both of which pieces have had enormous runs. As an actor he was, in many parts, unrivalled, more especially in Shakespearian characters, such as Sir Andrew Aguecheek, Touchstone, Master Slender, and he was equally successful as Bob Acres, Tony Lumpkin, Mawworm, Scrub, Marplot, and other leading characters in genuine legitimate comedy. In farces he was irresistibly comic, nor was he wanting in scenes of pathos or touches of nature. The drama lost one of its most favoured and most popular sons when poor Buckstone "shuffled off his mortal coil."

I was slightly acquainted with Charles Dibdin, the eldest son of the Ocean Bard, who was for many years a proprietor of Sadler's Wells Theatre, and author of the operas of "The Farmer's Wife," "My Spouse and I," and innumerable burlettas, songs, and pantomimes.

It is said that the elder Dibdin wrote above thirteen hundred songs—songs which were irresistible appeals to the heart, inspiring the most illiterate with brave and generous sentiments, and exciting to acts of loyalty, bravery, and patriotism, which (in the most arduous of her struggles) assisted to maintain the honour and glory of the British empire.

Prolific as was the father's pen, the son's produced nearly double the above mentioned number. Charles Dibdin died in 1831. With Thomas Dibdin, another son of the bard of "Poor Jack," I was intimately acquainted, and a more quaint, witty companion I never met. He was the author of "The English Fleet," "Mouth of the Nile," "Naval Pillar," "Nelson's Glory," and "The Cabinet." In the days of Braham and Storace "The English Fleet" and "The Cabinet" were two of the most popular operas, and for a length of time held possession of the operatic boards of Drury Lane and Covent Garden Theatres. His lines on Charles Dibdin's monument at Greenwich speak volumes for the kind heart of an affectionate son.

"Stop, shipmate, stop! He can't be dead,
   His lay yet lives to memory dear;

His spirit, merely shot ahead,
　　Will yet command Jack's smile and tear.
Still in my ear the songs resound,
　　That stemm'd the torrent at the Nore!
Avast! each hope of mirth's aground,
　　Should Charley be indeed no more.

"The evening watch, the sounding lead,
　　Will sadly miss old Charley's line,
Saturday night may go to bed,
　　His sun is set no more to shine.
'Sweethearts and Wives' though we may sing,
　　And toast, at sea, the girls on shore;
Yet now 'tis quite another thing,
　　Since Charley spins the yarn no more.

"Jack Rattlin's story now who'll tell?
　　Or chronicle each boatswain brave?
The sailor's kind historian fell
　　With him who sang the 'Soldier's Grave.'
'Poor Jack!' 'Ben Backstay!' but, belay!
　　Starboard and larboard, aft and fore,
Each from his brow may swab the spray,
　　Since tuneful Charley is no more.

"The capstan, compass, and the log
　　Will oft his Muse to memory bring;
And when all hands wheel round the grog,
　　They'll drink and blubber as they sing.
For grog was often Charley's theme,
　　A double spirit then it bore;
It sometimes seems to me a dream
　　That such a spirit is no more!

"It smooth'd the tempest, cheer'd the calm,
　　Made each a hero at his gun;
It even proved for foes a balm,
　　Soon as the angry fight was done.
Then, shipmate, check that rising sigh,
　　He's only gone ahead before;
For ever foremast men must die,
　　As well as Charley, now no more!"

Upon one occasion I received a letter from a lady with whom I was unacquainted, requesting an interview, upon a subject in which she considered I should take the deepest interest. The letter went on to say that the writer was most anxious to appear before a London audience in juvenile tragedy, and hoped I should so far oblige her as to hear her recite the part of Juliet. My reply was that, if she would favour me with a visit, I would invite Mr. Thomas Dibdin to meet her, he having it much more in his power to forward her wishes than I had.

The morning arrived, and, at the appointed hour, a lady closely veiled was ushered into the room. I rose and introduced my friend, Mr. Thomas Dibdin, at that period stage manager of one of the metropolitan theatres.

"From family circumstances, which I will not obtrude upon your lordship," mumbled the new-comer, in a low, almost inaudible voice, "I have been compelled to leave my father's house to seek my fortune on the London boards. My maiden modesty well may blush"—this was said in a high tragic tone—"at thus appearing at a young bachelor's house. My only request is that you will permit me during our interview to remain veiled."

"*Vale*," whispered Dibdin, who was an inveterate punster.

"I should be sorry," I replied, "to suggest anything that would be repugnant to your feelings; but I fear, if your face and features are hidden from our view, we shall not have so good an opportunity of judging of your histrionic powers as if you were unveiled."

"With a strict promise, then, that should you ever meet me in society you will not recognize me as having so far forgotten that delicacy which is due to my sex in thus calling upon you, I consent."

The promise was readily given, the lady unveiled, and I never saw a more beautiful or expressive countenance. Her hair was raven black, her eyes were dark, and her teeth were white as pearls. Her age appeared to be about twenty. When she took off her cloak, I saw that her figure was splendid, but more suited for such parts as Lady Macbeth and Volumnia than Juliet.

"Perhaps," said Dibdin, who I saw was evidently delighted with the looks of the aspirant for dramatic fame, "you would kindly go through the balcony scene; though not quite a Romeo myself, I will with pleasure read the part."

"Hi thank you," she replied.

I looked at Dibdin, who, like myself, seemed rather "taken aback" at the introduction of the letter H. Still I attributed it to nervousness. Placing herself behind an arm-chair, to represent the balcony, Miss —— (I will not mention the lady's name, though, after a period of half a century, I might be excused for so doing) began—Dibdin had given the cue, "that I might touch that cheek."

"Hah me!" was the reply.

This went on until she came to the speech, "Fain would I dwell on form," when, in an impassioned manner, she delivered it as follows,

> "Fain would hi dwell on form, fain, fain deny
> What hi 'ave spoke; but, farewell compliment.
> Dost thou love me? Hi know thou wilt say hay,
> And hi will take thy word."

Dibdin looked round at me, and wrote with a pencil on a scrap of paper, which he handed to me,

"Hi've 'eard enough. D—— her *I*'s."

There was more point than politeness in the remark, and I then turned over in my mind how, without wounding the young lady's feelings, I could put an end to the painful exhibition.

"Thank you," I replied, when she had finished the scene. "You possess many qualifications for an actress—a good stage appearance, an impassioned style, and evidently a devotion to the art; still, without wishing to dishearten you, I should strongly advise your placing yourself under some elocutionist."

"Helocutionist!" she replied, with a look of displeasure. "Hi consider hall hi want is practice."

Dibdin then came to my rescue, and, in a delicate and kindly manner, pointed out what he mildly called a "proprievalism," in her delivery of the words.

Miss —— rose with much dignity, and in a theatrical manner, exclaimed, quoting from Douglas,

"'I thank Glenalvon for his counsel, although it sounded harshly.'"

I heard no more of the lady until some months afterwards, when, in passing a small shop in St. Martin's Court, I espied "Juliet" measuring a yard of ribbon.

I often met Mark Lemon at the hospitable board of the late Mr. Tuxford, at that time proprietor of the *Mark Lane Express* and *New Sporting Magazine*. It was at his house that I became acquainted with the late Herbert Ingram, than whom a kinder-hearted man never existed. Ingram had got into some disfavour with a few of his constituents at Boston, and invited Tuxford, Mark Lemon, Shirley Brooks, and myself to accompany him to that borough, and do all in our power to remove the temporary inimical feeling that had been got up against him. Never shall I forget that visit. Mark Lemon and Shirley Brooks were in high spirits, and it is a wonder that I am alive to record the facts, when I say that, for two days before the grand political banquet in the Corn Exchange, we, after an early dinner of friends in Boston, attended three "oyster feasts," as they were called,—though it was a case of "Hamlet" without the Prince of Denmark, for oysters there were none, which feasts were kept up until near the time when the early village cock, "bright chanticleer, proclaims the morn."

I am here reminded of an anecdote which is attributed to the witty editor of *Punch*, Mark Lemon.

One evening, at a convivial party, Mark Lemon said:

"This is a better supper than old —— used to give the actors at —— in my early days. It was an actor's hostelry, and once a week they had a tripe supper. Some of the actors got tired of this plain fare, and one of them suggested a change in the same.

"'By all means,' said the host, and at the following meeting the actors and a few friends were present, myself amongst the number.

"Ushered into the dining-room, there were great demonstrations of preparation. The host in state on a raised seat at the further end of the table; by his side stood a servitor holding a herald's trumpet. The table was thickly covered with dishes. When we were all seated, the herald blew a flourish, and the host, in a loud voice, exclaimed,

"'Remove the covers, let the repast begin.'

"There were meats of all kinds—birds, chickens, game, tarts, fruits, everything we could think of; but they were the contents of a child's toy-box, wooden meats, wooden birds, painted apples. A cry of disgust, mingled with shouts of laughter, greeted this satire upon the actors' desire for luxuries. At the first burst of surprise, old —— in his loudest voice, said,

" ' Jim, bring in the tripe.'

"The wooden viands whetted the general appetite, and we spent a jovial evening."

Burnand I had the pleasure of meeting only once, and that was at Cromwell House, when he acted Puff in "The Critic." I have seen this part played by the two Mathews, father and son, by Jones, and by many professional and unprofessional actors; but no one, in my mind, came up to the present editor of *Punch*. There was no straining after effect, all seemed to come perfectly natural. There was no "gag," as it is termed, no attempt made to improve upon Sheridan; it was a perfect delineation of the character, and the happiest specimen of genuine, legitimate farce.

Byron I only know by reputation, but have always been delighted, not only with his dramatic works, but with his acting. There is an originality, a thorough knowledge of what the author means, and an attention to stage business which renders every part he undertakes faultless. However much the "100," "200," or "400" night system may be censured by those who seek for novelty, an author cannot fail to be gratified when he finds the public flocking to the theatre to witness the extraordinary run his piece has had. This gratification must be felt to the greatest degree by the subject of this brief memoir. Few men have written so much, or to such purpose, as Byron.

Palgrave Simpson is an excellent fellow, and what is familiarly termed "good company." He is an admirable amateur actor, and a first-rate dramatic writer. People are very often apt to judge of an actor, whether professional or unprofessional, by the effect produced by the character he undertakes, and not by the correct delineation he imparts to it. Some characters, as the phrase goes, "act themselves," and, with the slightest aid of histrionic talent, are rendered prominent. The great difficulty is to make much of an up-hill part, and it requires more than ordinary talent and assiduity to create any interest in it.

This talent Palgrave Simpson possesses to a great degree, and whether the part he undertakes is heavy, dreary, monotonous, or repugnant to the feelings of the audience, it will always form a prominent feature. As a dramatic writer, Palgrave Simpson knows precisely how to suit the taste of the public; he selects powerful incidents, characters out of the ordinary line, and clothes them with language vigorous, refined, or humorous, as the situation requires.

Barham Livius, who wrote an amusing piece entitled "Maid or Wife," was always introduced at a dinner or evening party as "Baron Livius,' whether through the mistake of the servant, or, what was more likely, through his giving his name so as to sound like Baron, I know not. Still it did appear strange that all servants should fall into the same error. After a time he became, or at least claimed to be, a German baron, and was then universally recognised as one. He organised a theatrical company to perform English plays in Holland, but the scheme entirely failed, and justly so, for the *corps dramatique* was a very ordinary one. Upon their return to England, loud was the cry against the baron, and law-suits were threatened. The ladies of this untoward expedition, who were really clever artists, and who had sacrificed many other engagements in England, were, like the widows of Ashur, " loud in their wail." I rather think the baron retired to his German estate, probably a sort of " château en Espagne."

Henry R. Addison, who only died a few years ago, and with whom I was well acquainted, wrote " The Moon's Age," " The King's Word," and "Tam o' Shanter" with tolerable success; he also produced a piece at the Adelphi Theatre, called " The Butterfly's Ball," founded on the beautiful poem of that name.

It was during the period that Mrs. Honey was enchanting all by her beauty and talent. One day, after a dinner at the " Old Garrick," I suggested the subject, thinking that lady would look to perfection as the Butterfly. We talked the matter over, and I furnished one or two of the lines and songs, but they were not of importance enough to give me a title to joint authorship. The piece, thanks to splendid scenery, pretty women, and becoming dresses, was fairly successful.

CHAPTER VI.

THE LATE LORD LYTTON—"PAUL CLIFFORD"—OVATION TO THE AUTHOR—THE VICTORIA THEATRE—BYRON—GUICCIOLI—HER APPRECIATION OF "CHILDE HAROLD"—RAIKES AND THE DANDIES—JUDGE TALFOURD—MRS. CHARLES GORE—HAYNES BAYLEY—"I'D BE A BUTTERFLY"—ENTHUSIASM OF THE WRITER OF IT.

> Les rimeurs sont nombreux, les poètes sont rare.
> LA HARPE.

I NOW approach dramatic writers, wholly unconnected with the theatre, who have produced some of our best sterling tragedies and comedies, with all of whom I was on terms of the greatest friendship. Let me commence with the late Lord Lytton, who, as Bulwer Lytton, produced unquestionably the best dramas of the present day, notably "The Lady of Lyons," "Money," and "Richelieu," all of which have remained great favourites with the public at large.

In 1837 "La Duchesse de la Vallière" was produced at Covent Garden Theatre, and, although it failed from the story being one for which it was difficult to enlist the sympathies of an English audience, it contained some beautiful lines, which none but a poet of the highest order could have conceived and embodied.

Many delightful hours did I pass in the society of Bulwer Lytton at his cottage, some few miles from London. His unaffected manner, his kindness of heart, his amiable disposition, setting aside his gigantic talents as an orator, a poet, a prose writer, and a dramatist, endeared him to all who came within the circle of his acquaintance; and I shall ever look back with the deepest gratitude to the distinguished privilege of being included in the list of his friends. He was as good in all the generous impulses of social intercourse as he was great in the more onerous duties of a statesman.

One day, when meeting him at the house of a common acquaintance, with whom he was on intimate terms, it was suggested that we should all meet again at an early dinner, and proceed to the Victoria Theatre to witness the representation of "Paul Clifford," which had recently been dramatised. Upon reaching the box-entrance we were told that there was not a place to be had, not even standing room. This was a great compliment to the author of the novel, who seemed highly pleased. Not liking to be thwarted, I sent in my card to the manager, who at once received me in his private room. After congratulating him on the success of "Paul Clifford," I informed him that Mr. and Mrs. Bulwer and another lady were waiting in the entrance-hall, anxious to find places.

"I'll see what I can do," said the manager. "My own private box is occupied; but I will try to get my friends places in the orchestra."

This was accordingly done, and we soon took possession of the vacant box, the manager declining to receive any remuneration for it.

The drama was admirably well acted, and Bulwer—for he had not then attained that rank which his eminent talents entitled him to—was in a state of frantic delight. At the conclusion all eyes were turned on the box, and in a second the whole audience rose *en masse* to cheer the principal occupier of it. At first Bulwer shrank back, but we pressed him to go forward, and when he appeared in front he received a perfect ovation.

I have been present during royal and imperial visits in England, France, Austria, Bavaria, Holland, and Belgium, but I never heard such enthusiastic shouts as were given to the author of "Paul Clifford" upon the above occasion.

In early life, when a boy at Westminster, I met Lord Byron at his "corporeal pastor's" sparring-rooms in Bond Street, and had the pleasure of dining in company with him upon two occasions, and accompanying him to the committee box at Drury Lane Theatre, of which he was a member.

After the play, which was during Edmund Kean's successful engagement, we supped with Sir Godfrey Webster at "Long's Hotel." It was then the noble bard shone pre-eminently great; all reserve was thrown aside, and for hours he delighted us with anecdotes of the green-room, the subjects of which are passed away and long forgotten.

While upon the subject of Byron, I cannot refrain from mentioning that upon more than one occasion I had the pleasure of meeting that "fair-haired daughter" of Italia, Teresa Gamba, Countess Guiccioli. There can be no doubt that Guiccioli was the real object of Childe Harold's devotion. What can be more tender than the following lines written by him:—

"In that word, *amor mio*, is comprised my existence here and hereafter. Think of me sometimes when the Alps and the ocean divide us—but they never will, unless you wish it."

Of him, too, she wrote, after her first introduction:—

"La nobile e bellissima sua pronomia, il suono della sua voce, le sue maniere, e mille incanti che lo circondavano, lo rendevano un essere cosi differente, cosi superiore a tutti quelli che io aveva sin' allora veduti, che non potéi a mano di non provarne la piu profonda impressione."

The Countess's manner was perfectly charming. No wonder, then, that she held such sway over the heart of the noble poet.

In the *Revue de Paris,* a clever writer, M. Jules Janin, pays the following tribute to Byron, in a commentary on his life and writings. After comparing his genius to that of Homer, Virgil, and Tasso, he asserts that "déclamé ou chanté, Iliade ou Odyssée, 'Childe Harold' est toujours le poème unique des temps modernes."

M. Janin represents Byron as a most interesting, romantic, and persecuted character, foiled in his noble political pursuits at home by a prejudiced, despotic ministry; depreciated and criticised with the bitterest satire by his literary contemporaries; calumniated and driven from society by the unfeeling acrimony of false friends, and the prejudiced coteries of fashionable life; and at last seeking a refuge in foreign climes against the cruel persecution of an unjust and ungrateful country.

There can be no doubt that there is a great deal of truth in the above eulogium, and I feel very much disposed to follow the example of the elector of Bristol who, after listening to one of Burke's most splendid speeches, exclaimed, "And I say ditto to all Mr. Burke has said," altering the words of "Mr. Burke" to those of M. Janin.

Raikes, in his journal, thus comments on the above, with, I think, extreme bad taste:—

"Now this is all very well for French romance, but everyone who knows the real position of Lord Byron must be aware that there is not one syllable of truth in it. His lot was that of any other modern English gentleman, who prefers his pleasures to his duties, and seeks for happiness where it never can be found, in the wayward indulgence of his own caprice."

Surely the above does not come with very

good grace from one who, on his return to England from a tour abroad, "became a partner in his father's house; but having little inclination for mercantile affairs, and a marked preference for social pursuits, very soon established himself in the West End of the town, became a member of the fashionable clubs, and mixed largely in what is, by a somewhat questionable courtesy, denominated the *best* society."

He thus proceeds:

"Notwithstanding his great talents—and no one can wish to deny them—he was a selfish, and, at times, a dissipated character; he married a valuable woman, whom he treated with cruelty and neglect. Occupied with his Muse, whom, to gratify private spleen, he would occasionally arm with the bitterest weapons, he never attempted to obtain any celebrity in the politics or the senate of his country, where so wide a field was open to his exertions and endowments.

"At length, because his captious vanity was indignant at the common criticism of his early productions, which no author can escape, and his pride was hurt at some natural comments on his character as a husband, he flies in disgust to the continent, vowing hatred and enmity to every unfortunate English idler whom he may meet on his travels, affecting what he calls

> 'That vital scorn of all,
> As if the worst had fallen that could befall,'

and trying to dupe the world with the mask of

> 'The man of loneliness and mystery;
> Scarce seen to smile, and seldom heard to sigh!'

"His romantic admirers on the continent have at length canonized him as a martyr to calumny and oppression; while those who remember certain dinners at Watier's in the olden time, and certain long potations with John Kemble, Brummell, and other *virtuosi*, have no faith in the affected misanthropy, and only recollect an agreeable companion—the *bon convive qui boit sec*.

"Lord Byron might have remained with perfect ease and security in his native country, if his own restless spirit would have permitted it; he might have reaped every honour from his talents in the senate, or his poetical pursuits in the closet, and, notwithstanding the faults which he complains were so unjustly visited upon him, he might have been what he pleased in society, the idol or the tyrant of the *grand monde.*

"The time is long gone by (and daily examples prove it) when vice or misconduct could serve to exclude a man of rank and fashion from the highest and most distinguished circles in London."

This severe hit at the society in which Raikes lived appears strange from one whose highest ambition was to become a leader of *ton.*

But Raikes was ever cantankerous and disagreeable. One day, at White's window, he was what is termed "chaffing" D'Orsey about an anonymous letter the latter had received sealed with a wafer-stamp.

"I think," said the count, turning to Lord (commonly called King) Allen, "Raikes himself must have written it, and sealed it with his nose;" thus referring to the nasal organ of the journalist, which was pitted with the small-pox.

It was rather ungrateful of Raikes to attack Byron, inasmuch as the noble lord thus speaks of the dandies, of which his libeller aspired to take the deposed sovereign, Brummell's, place:

"The dandies, as a body, were harmless, good-natured men. Brummell, despite his absurdities, was a very agreeable companion, and might have turned his talents, which were great, to a better account. To denounce a man for 'malting' when he asked for a glass of beer; to tell his neighbour, when asked if he liked vegetables, that he sometimes 'indulged in a pea,' were quoted as clever sayings; from anyone else they would have been looked upon as very silly remarks."

The story of "Wales, ring the bell," is not true, but Brummell did inquire "Who is your fat friend?" The circumstance occurred at a ball given by four of the "Exclusives" to the Prince of Wales and a large party. As His Royal Highness entered the room he pointedly passed Brummell, who coolly turned to Sir Harry Mildmay, one of the ball-givers, and asked, " Who is your fat friend ?"

I passed a day at Calais with the Beau, after his star had set, but he was, as ever, delightful and brilliant.

Raikes I have already referred to. Sir Harry Mildmay was a well informed man, and universally popular. John Mills, the Mosaic dandy, as he was called, was rather pompous, but not devoid of good qualites. Alvanley was excellent company, his wit was brilliant, sharp, and polished, and he carefully avoided personalities. Edward Montagu, afterwards Lord Rokeby, was clever and agreeable. Rufus Lloyd had very little to distinguish him from the rest of mankind, with the exception of being what Freeman, in "High Life Below Stairs," calls "very carrotty in the poll." "King Allen" was very amiable when not attacked by his only enemy, the gout.

Judge Talfourd, the author of "Ion," must not be omitted in my catalogue of dramatic celebrities, nor must his agreeable and clever son, who wrote some of the best burlesques that have appeared on the stage,—notably that of "Ixion,"—be passed over. He came next to Byron and Burnand in that particular department of dramatic literature; the latter two have taken a higher flight, and have produced comedies that would rank with those of Sheridan, Colman, Morton, and Reynolds. I had the pleasure of constantly meeting the judge, as Serjeant Talfourd, and Judge Talfourd, at the old Garrick Club, at his house in Russell Square, and on the Circuit, and a more genial, kindhearted, agreeable man I never met. Of his talents as a lawyer I need not speak, for they won for him world-wide reputation; but as a companion at the festive board, as host of a small part of his learned legal brethren, as manager of his private theatricals, when "Ion" was splendidly got up at his mansion in Russell Square, as doing the honours of a supper after the play, surrounded by men eminent at the bar, in literature, in art, in science, in politics, Judge Talfourd was second to none.

Talfourd's dramatic works include "Ion," "The Athenian Captive," "Glencoe," and "The Castilian." In addition to which he wrote "The Life of Charles Lamb," "Vacation Rambles," and a "Biography of Mrs. Radcliffe."

Thomas Noon Talfourd received the rudiments of his education at the Grammar School at Mill Hill, in which establishment he was placed in the year 1809. He remained at the Grammar School about five years. At a very early period of his life he was fond of declamation; his school-fellows would rally round him to hear some humorous invectives against political questions of moment, or commendations of particular plans in which his youthful enterprises were involved and his eloquence enforced.

His delivery was characterised by great rapidity, his language was extremely copious, his imagination was lively, his descriptive powers were superb, and the method he adopted to illustrate his subject was most felicitous, yet natural and unstudied. These qualities, though matured by age, were conspicuous in him during his life.

After leaving Mill Hill he entered Dr. Valpy's school at Reading, where he remained until he was sixteen or seventeen. His progress and advancement while under the doctor's roof were brilliant in the extreme. On leaving Dr. Valpy's school he did not proceed to the university, but immediately commenced his studies for the bar under a very able special pleader. This employment brought him into contact with many of the leading performers—Macready, Munden, and the elder Mathews.

It was feared by some, at this period of his life, that his love of theatrical acquaintances would operate prejudicially to his studies for the bar; for the above and many other leading actors were his constant visitors at his chambers in the Temple. After a time he found it necessary to relax his taste for the histrionic art, and pursue with vigour that profession in which he was so eminently qualified to excel. This resolution he scrupulously carried out.

Shortly after Mr. Talfourd was called to the bar, he married a very amiable and accomplished lady. In due course of time he became a Serjeant-at-Law, and finally a judge. A more honourable, upright, just, intelligent, and moral man could not have been selected for a post so onerous and responsible.

I now approach less brilliant dramatic writers; still their talents merit a small niche in the Temple of Fame.

I often met in society, where she was a distinguished member, Mrs. Charles Gore, who won the prize for the best comedy, offered by the manager of the Haymarket. As a novelist she took high rank, and must have felt pride in carrying off the dramatic trophy I have referred to. Few ladies were more gifted with conversational powers than Mrs. Charles Gore; her liveliness, and cleverness, and unaffected manner gained her, most deservedly, a legion of friends.

Haynes Bailey, commonly called "Butterfly Bailey," from his popular song of "I'd be a Butterfly," was more of a sonneteer than a dramatic writer. A farce of his, "Perfection, or the Lady of Munster," still holds possession of the stage. It is a great favourite with amateurs.

I knew Bailey well, and passed many pleasant days in the company of himself and his pretty little wife at Bath. I also met him at Boulogne, on my way to Paris, and being pressed by him to remain there for a day or two to talk over old times I most gladly consented

Never shall I forget an incident that occurred there. I was walking on the pier with him when all of a sudden an itinerant organ-player struck up, though rather inharmoniously, the air of "I'd be a Butterfly." He suddenly stopped, gasped for breath, seemed for a moment uncertain whether it was his "Butterfly," and then exclaimed, in a voice that might be heard by all around him,

"It is my 'Butterfly!'"

"Flown across the channel," I said, "to do honour to its composer in France."

Wellington after Waterloo, Sheridan after his celebrated "Warren Hastings' speech" in Westminster Hall, Edmund Kean after his triumph, when, at the conclusion of his performance of Richard the Third, the entire pit rose and cheered him, Angelina d'Atti after receiving showers of bouquets for her inimitable singing in " La Sonnambula," could not have felt prouder than Haynes Bailey did at this unexpected compliment to his musical genius.

CHAPTER VII.

AMATEURS, GENERALLY SPEAKING, NOT ACTORS—EXCEPTION TO THE ABOVE RULE—FREDERICK YATES—PRESCOTT, ROYAL ARTILLERY—COLE, 21ST FUSILEERS—BENSON HILL, ROYAL ARTILLERY—FRACAS WITH A' FRENCH AUDIENCE AT VALENCIENNES—ARTHUR CECIL—CORNEY GRAIN—COLLETTE—ALEXANDER KYRLE BELLEW—THE HON. MRS. WROTTESLEY—THE HON. LADY SEBRIGHT—LADY MONCKTON—MRS. BERENS.

> Best of all madrigals,
> Private theatricals;
> All that we want is to settle the play.
> JAMES SMITH.

AMATEUR acting is now the rage; but in the present, as in bygone days, few amateurs are good enough to transfer their services to the regular boards. There were, however, some honourable exceptions, and perhaps the most brilliant one was in the person of Frederick Yates, who, from the Commissariat Department, became a first-rate actor.

His first appearance in private was at the Château Mont St. Martin, near Cambray, rented by the late Duke of Wellington during the occupation of the allied army in France after the battle of Waterloo. Here, in company with Mathews the elder, Yates gave an entertainment which was highly successful. Shortly after he came to London, and, the staff of the Commissariat Department being reduced, he turned his thoughts to the stage, to which he became a distinguished ornament both as actor and manager.

Prescott, of the Royal Artillery, joined the professional corps, and appeared under the *nom de théâtre* of Ward. He was a very gentlemanlike-looking and highly-polished mannered man, and acquitted himself extremely well, if not in the first, at least in the second rank of tragedians.

Cole, who appeared as Calcraft, I have already referred to.

Last, not least, was Benson Hill of the Artillery, who acted a Frenchman to perfection. Never shall I forget the impression he made as Bagatello in "The Poor Soldier" at Valenciennes, at an amateur play got up by the English officers quartered in that town, or the disgust which the French portion of the audience felt at what they considered a caricature on their countrymen. Indeed, from the anger displayed by a resident of that town, it was fortunate for Benson Hill that he was not challenged to mortal combat. Many a duel, in some cases fatal, arose from much more trivial causes. Had it not been for the tact and discretion of a brother-officer, poor Benson might have received a bullet in the "thorax," or a thrust of a small sword in the heart.

It was said—whether true or false I know not—that Benson Hill's physiognomy was so formed by nature that he never could laugh, and only showed by his eyes and open mouth that he felt jocularly inclined. He wrote a book on snuff-taking, which gained some celebrity at the time. Whether a pinch of that pungent powder, manufactured by Lundy Foot, "Irish Blackguard," as it was irreverently called, would have caused the muscles of his face to relax, I am not informed. All I can vouch for is that nothing could be more comical than his countenance when trying in vain to give way to laughter.

At the present time many amateurs have given up acting, under the cloak of charity, before a partial audience, and have boldly claimed the suffrages of the public, and in every instance the success that has attended them has been complete.

Arthur Cecil has proved himself to be an artist of the highest order. I doubt much whether, in the line he has selected, he has ever been equalled; quite sure am I that he has never been surpassed. Here, although I may lay myself open to the charge of egotism while indulging in the offensive pronoun *I*, I cannot refrain from saying that, however I may fail in other qualities, I possess that of discernment, more especially as regards acting.

Some years ago, when the Bijou Theatre

was open in the old Italian Opera House in the Haymarket, I attended an amateur performance to witness "The Rivals," in which the part of Mrs. Malaprop was represented by the Honourable Mrs. Wrottesley, unquestionably the best lady actress of that or any other day. I forget the names of the others; suffice it to say that, for amateurs, they acquitted themselves extremely well. There was one among them, however, with whom I was much struck, and I turned to my brother-in-law, the late Lord De Ros, and remarked, "That's an actor."

This was Arthur Cecil, who acted the small part of the boy whom Fag kicks downstairs. He has only a few words to say, but those words he said with such point and intelligence as at once to stamp him as an actor. In addition to which his action, his by-play, were so complete that I felt convinced, if ever he contemplated making the stage his profession, he would become a distinguished ornament to it.

Corney Grain also claims honourable mention. Had he stuck to the legal profession, he would probably have shone as much at the bar as a barrister, as he has as an actor and singer before the bar of public opinion. He, however, appears to have preferred the study of parts to the reading of briefs, the stage costume to the robe and wig, singing to pleading, play-bills to parchment, St. George's Hall to the Court of Queen's Bench, a theatrical tour to an Oxford Circuit, a certain retaining "fee" every Saturday from the treasury to an uncertain one in chambers, a "refresher" at the south coast to one in the dense atmosphere of Chancery Lane, a round of applause from an overflowing house to a murmur of approbation, suddenly suppressed by the august mandate, "Silence—I'll order the Court to be cleared," the green-room to the robing-room in Westminster Hall, approval to "demurrers," and, above all, the delight of appealing to an enlightened public, instead of addressing a common or special jury. If the legal profession have lost a clever counsel, the public have gained a most talented actor.

The name of Collette may be fairly added to the above roll. As Paul Pry, partly re-written by him, he is inimitable, and the response to his appeal, "I hope I don't intrude," would be "Such intrusions are delightful, pray continue them."

Mr. Alexander (I give his theatrical name), who distinguished himself as an amateur, has made a great sensation on the regular boards as a *jeune première*, a *rôle* very difficult to fill, but for which his good looks and gentlemanlike manners eminently qualify him.

Mr. Kyrle Bellew, son of one of the most talented elocutionists of the day, commenced his public career by following in his father's steps. Since that he has devoted his energies to the stage, and has proved himself to be second to none in light comedy parts. His Orlando in "As You Like It" was an admirable performance, perfectly natural, and free from what is technically called "staginess." I may have omitted the names of others equally deserving a place among amateurs, who have made the stage their profession and have won histrionic honours, but my object has been to confine my remarks to those amateurs whose performances I have witnessed.

There can be no doubt that highly-educated women and men would, with study and practice, become excellent actresses and actors, and we could name many that, if transported from the performances of a drawing-room, or private theatre, to the regular boards, would command salaries. Let me name the Honourable Mrs. Wrottesley, whose acting is faultless; the Honourable Lady Sebright, full of genius, *verve*, and energy; Lady Monckton, graceful, pathetic, tender, joyous, and thoroughly acquainted with the business of the stage; Mrs. Berens, handsome and majestic, who as Queen Constance, and other Shakespearian characters, would captivate all hearts; Mrs. Theobald, touching and pathetic; Miss Williams, pretty and pleasing. There are other young ladies who, with deep study and intense practice, would become worthy of the regular boards, but who now wish to run before they can walk, who think that the requirements of an *artiste* consist in, parrot-like, learning the words of the part allotted them.

Among the men there are many who would prove great acquisitions to the regular boards, but it would be invidious to select any. Suffice it then to say the "Old Stagers" and "The Windsor Strollers" could furnish a large number capable of holding their own with professionals.

CHAPTER VIII.

MUSICAL TASTE IN ENGLAND GREATLY IMPROVED—VERDI—
HIS LIFE, HIS STRUGGLES, HIS BRILLIANT SUCCESS.

No man's abilities are so remarkably shining as not to stand in need of a proper opportunity, a patron, and even the praises of a friend to recommend them to the notice of the world.

PLINY.

THERE can be no doubt that the taste for music has increased wonderfully within the last fifty years, and there are few countries in which the best operatic and classical music can be heard to better advantage than in our own.

Two Italian Opera Houses seem to thrive while formerly one only existed, and that with scant remuneration to the lessee. In addition to which we have an Opera Comique, a Globe, and an Alhambra where the most popular compositions of Offenbach and others are heard to the greatest advantage.

Mozart, Rossini, Meyerbeer, Donizetti, Flotow, Gounod, and Verdi still hold their potent spell over the hearts of the lovers of music, and no one more so than the last-mentioned composer, of whom I am about to speak. His career, by turns so depressing, so brilliant, cannot fail to interest the reader, as it proves that, by patient struggles and steady perseverance, difficulties may be overcome, and a man, possessing the above qualities, may raise himself from the humblest to the highest position in his profession.

Giuseppe Verdi was born at Bonsole, in the Duchy of Parma, in the year 1814. An inn of no great pretensions witnessed his birth and his fame. Here he listened to the rural songs of those rustic travellers who were accustomed to assemble in the public room of the small caravansary.

At the church of this small village the organist was in the habit not only of playing sacred music on Sundays and Saints' days, but indulged in his favourite pursuit whenever he was enabled to spend an hour from his usual avocations.

To these performances the young Verdi would listen with the deepest attention; so much so that the organist took him by the hand, and imparted to him all the musical knowledge he possessed.

One of the earliest dreams of the youthful Giuseppe was, at some future period, to become the organist of the village church. In the meantime he took the greatest delight in light music, whether played by itinerant barrel-organists or by a military band.

His love of light, especially dancing, music drew down some severe comments from a celebrated professor of Italian music, who denounced Giuseppe Verdi as "obstinate, ugly, and so eccentric that he preferred dancing music to classical works."

Fortunately for Verdi, Antonio Barezzi, a

rich amateur and lover of music, was so enchanted with his talent that he promised to procure for him an entrance to the Conservatoire at Milan. Here, however, Francesco Basili, one of those prejudiced pedagogues who think none but their own *protégés* possess any musical talent, declared Verdi to be unworthy of a place in the Conservatoire, and declined to admit him.

Basili was not himself devoid of talent as a composer of some sacred and operatic music, but he was very authoritative. He, however, laid himself open to the greatest ridicule in dismissing the young aspirant for fame, whom he pronounced to understand nothing, to know nothing, to feel nothing, but who eventually gained the highest pinnacle in the temple of fame, as the composer of "Rigoletto," in which the far-famed quartett remains a brilliant gem without a flaw, and of "Aida," which revived the splendour of Italian Lyrics.

Rejected by Basili, Verdi, not at all disconcerted, renounced the Institutions, and turned his thoughts to the theatre of La Scala, where

Lavigna had become celebrated as a pianist. Under his tuition he studied, and became thoroughly acquainted with the works of Mozart.

One evening, at a concert of the Philharmonic Society, when the subject of Mozart was being discussed by the artists and amateurs, Verdi was called upon to execute some of this grand maestro's passages, which he did with his accustomed verve. At its conclusion a gentleman approached him in a hurried manner, and drew from his pocket-book a card on which was inscribed the name of Mozart. This led to a friendly shake of the hand, the stranger proving to be a son of Mozart, who was employed in the Austrian custom-house. From this hour Verdi was condemned to devote himself entirely to the music of the celebrated composer of "Don Giovanni."

Upon his emancipation from his maestro, Lavigna, Verdi composed many military marches, serenades, and patriotic songs, which, though condemned by Basili, received the warmest eulogies from Lavigna. After a time Verdi produced an opera, which met with the most perfect success. He was congratulated as the national composer of Italy, and Basili was bound to acknowledge that he had been guilty of the greatest mistake in underrating the talents of one who would have proved his most distinguished pupil. His second opera was equally successful, and was received with enthusiasm, while "Nabuco," his third composition, stamped him at once as the musical genius of the day. In the month of February, 1843, "I Lombardi" was produced at the Opera House, Milan, and created a perfect furore, so great, indeed, that the cognoscenti no longer talked of Bellini, Donizetti, Rossini, or Meyerbeer.

In March, 1844, "Ernani" was brought out, an opera in which the composer exerted his best energies; the result was the most unqualified success, not only in Italy, but throughout Europe. The libretto was originally from the prolific pen of Victor Hugo, but was afterwards altered by Verdi, the scene being transferred from Spain to Italy, and a new title suggested, that of "Il Prosaretto." The latter idea was abandoned, and the opera retained its original title, "Ernani." "I due Foscari" succeeded "Ernani," and was played at Rome; it was followed by "Alzira," performed at Naples, "Attila," represented at Venice, and "Macbeth," which met with the greatest applause, at Florence. "Aida," Verdi's master-piece, brought down some severe criticisms for having avoided the plaintive melodies which are usually given to heroines, and introduced accents violent and tragic. If Verdi was justly open to these bitter remarks, Mozart, Glück in "Alceste" and "Iphigénie en Tauride," Spontini, Meyerbeer, Rossini, not to omit Wagner and De Berlioz, were equally to blame, for in their operas we have energetic heroines—nay, savage ones.

At Paris Verdi set his face against the "Claque," for which he was highly applauded by the celebrated "George Sand." I give her *nom de plume.*

"Verdi," she remarked, "possesses genius of the highest order; he has a noble heart, despises the applause paid in advance according to a tariff; he requires no claque—the public are to him the claque."

During one of the last representations of "Les Vêpres Siciliennes," he was told that the house was not half filled. In a corner sat a man who appeared to be thoroughly attentive, and was taking notes of the performance. The director of the Opera House, having ascertained that this man was head of the "claqueurs," suggested to Verdi the expediency of engaging his services. A frown came over the composer's countenance, as he exclaimed, in a satirical tone,

"Of the 'claque,' this national police of the French theatres, I know nothing, and highly disapprove of it. What is it to me? I hold no communication with it."

To prove how little he cared for this hired applause will be seen by the following anecdote. A song by the tenor at the end of an act was always enthusiastically received; the composer, however, considered that a better termination would be produced by a recitative.

"Why," asked the "Impressario," "do you not let the curtain drop on that splendid air which always creates such a sensation, and is unanimously applauded?"

"But suppose it was not applauded?"

"Then they might hiss."

"Well, then I should be hissed."

A contrary effect, however, was produced.

The first representation of "La Jerusalem" took place at Paris on the 20th of November, 1847, and it was most favourably received. Verdi, like Rossini, was conspicuous for the religious feeling which both of the above composers introduced into some of their operas. What can exceed the deep feeling, the exquisite grace, when, in "Nabuco," the Jews sing a hymn on their captivity :—

"Va, pensiero sull'ale dorate,
Va, ti posa sui divi, sui colli,
Ove olezzano libere e molli,
L'aure dolce del suolo natal."

In our "mind's eye" we see the captives shedding tears on quitting their beloved country, and their sadness in this valley of mourning. Rossini was equally sublime and touching in his "Moïse."

CHAPTER IX.

DRAMATIC LITERATURE—CONGREVE—YOUNG—GAY—ADDISON—THOMSON—RICHARD CUMBERLAND—HOLCROFT.

La comédie est l'art d'enseigner la vertu et les bienséances en actions et en dialogues.
VOLTAIRE.

BEFORE I turn to the French stage, which may be considered as having brought forward some of the best tragedies and some of the best comedies, it may not be out of place to refer to those English writers whose works, in their day, produced the greatest effect; few of which, however, would suit the taste of the present generation in our more refined times, owing to the immorality of their plots and the indecency, nay, coarseness, of their language.

Thus few of Congreve's plays are suited to the refined taste of modern audiences. "Love for Love," which at one time was a most popular comedy, when revived some years ago at one of the winter theatres, failed to attract, although the pruning-knife, liberally applied, had cut off many excrescences, and the dialogue had been carefully cleansed of its indecencies.

Congreve's first dramatic work was "The Old Bachelor," written, as the author says, "to amuse himself in a slow recovery from a fit of sickness, and with little thoughts of having it produced on the stage." Considering the age of the writer, it is in truth a wonderful production; for, whenever written, it was acted in 1693, when he was not more than twenty-one years old. Its success was unequivocal, proving highly beneficial, as it procured him the patronage of Halifax, who appointed him to several remunerative posts in the Customs and other offices. "The Double-Dealer" was not so successful, although Queen Mary honoured both the above-mentioned plays by her presence.

In 1695 "Love for Love" was produced, and received with the greatest favour. Congreve's last play, "The Way of the World," was received with so little favour that he resolved never again to submit his fame to the caprices of an audience. His tragedy of "The Mourning Bride" proved that the author was qualified for either kind of dramatic poetry. As Monimia Mrs. Siddons was pre-eminently great. Since her day the play has seldom been performed.

It appears that a tragedy by Young, entitled "Busiris," was brought out at Drury Lane in 1719. It was inscribed to the Duke of Newcastle in the following dedication:—"Because the late instances he had received of his Grace's undeserved and uncommon favour, in an affair of some consequence, foreign to the theatre, had taken from him the privilege of choosing a patron."

"Busiris" was followed, in the year 1731, by "The Revenge." He dedicated this tragedy to the Duke of Wharton.

"Your Grace," he says, "has been pleased to make yourself accessory to the following scenes, not only by suggesting the most beautiful incident in them, but by making all possible provision for the success of the whole."

That his Grace may have suggested the incident to which the author alludes is not unlikely. The last mental creation of the superannuated young man, at Lerida, in Spain, was some scenes of a tragedy on the story of Mary Queen of Scots.

Upon Young entering into orders, his tragedy of "The Brothers," which was in rehearsal, was withdrawn by him, much to the reluctance of the manager, but in deference to the new clergyman.

"Busiris" never kept its hold on the public; it was too remote from real life to raise either grief, terror, or indignation. "The Revenge" approaches much nearer to human practices and manners, and has therefore kept possession of the stage.

Although Gay wrote the tragedy of "The Captives," and a comedy called "The Wife of Bath," and another entitled "Three Hours after Marriage," his dramatic fame would have sunk into insignificance had he not produced "The Beggar's Opera." Honoured by command of the Princess of Wales to read "The Captives" before her, when the hour arrived he saw the Princess and her ladies all in expectation, and, advancing with reverence too great for any other attention, stumbled at a chair, and, falling forward, threw down a weighty Japan screen. The Princess started, the ladies screamed, and poor Gay, after all this confusion and disturbance, was still to read the play.

"The Captives" was acted at Drury Lane in 1723—4, for seven nights. The author's third night was under the patronage of the Prince and Princess of Wales. Previous to the above, Gay brought "The Wife of Bath" upon the stage; it was attended with small success.

Seventeen years after, having altered it to suit, as he thought, the taste of the public, he again brought it forward, but had the mortification to see it again rejected.

Gay was also the author of a mock tragedy, entitled "What D'ye Call It?" an agreeable trifle, which gave pleasure by its novelty, and proved tolerably successful. The author's great triumph was "The Beggar's Opera." This play, written to ridicule the musical Italian drama, was first offered to Cibber and his brethren at Drury Lane, and rejected; it was then carried to Rich, and had the effect, as was cleverly said, " of making Gay *rich* and Rich *gay*. Congreve, after reading it over, said "that it would either take greatly or be damned confoundedly." Happily for the author the first prediction was realized.

Its reception is thus recorded in the notes of the "Dunciad":—

"This piece was received with greater applause than was ever known. Besides being acted in London sixty-three nights without interruption, and renewed the next season with equal applause, it spread into all the great towns of England, was played in many places to the thirtieth and fortieth time; at Bath and Bristol fifty, &c. It made its progress into Wales, Scotland, and Ireland, where it was performed twenty-four nights successively. The ladies carried about with them the favourite songs of it in fans, and houses were furnished with it in screens. The fame of it was not confined to the author only. The person who acted Polly, till then obscure, became all at once the favourite of the town; her pictures were engraved, and sold in great numbers, her life written, books of letters and verses to her published, and pamphlets made even of her sayings and jests. Furthermore, it drove out of England (for that season) the Italian opera, which had carried all before it for ten years."

Of this performance, when it was printed, the reception was different according to the different opinions of the readers. Swift commended it for the excellence of its morality, as a piece that placed all kinds of vice in the strongest and most odious light; others—among them Dr. Herring, afterwards Archbishop of Canterbury—censures it severely, as giving encouragement not only to vice but to crimes, by making a highwayman the hero, and dismissing him at last unpunished. It has been even said that, after the exhibition of "The Beggar's Opera," the gang of robbers was evidently multiplied.

This objection, however, or some other, probably more political than moral, obtained such prevalence that, when Gay produced a second part under the name of "Polly," it was prohibited by the Lord Chamberlain. A subscription was got up to console the author, which was so liberally bestowed that what he looked upon as oppression ended in profit. The publication of "Polly" also produced the author a considerable sum. As a further recompence for the supposed hardship he had undergone he received the affectionate attentions of the Duke and Duchess of Queensbury, into whose house he was taken, and with whom he passed the remaining part of his life. After his death his opera of "Achilles" was acted, and the profits were given to two widowed sisters, his lawful heirs. There also appeared, under his name, a comedy called "The Distressed Wife" and "The Rehearsal at Gotham," a piece of humour, the fate of which is not known.

In my early play-going days Addison's "Cato" was a popular, albeit, according to my weak judgment, a very dull tragedy. According to Dr. Johnson, when "Cato" was shown to Pope, he advised the author to print it, without any theatrical exhibition, supposing that it would be read more favourably than heard. Addison declared himself of the same opinion, but urged the importunity of his friends for its appearance on the stage. The emulation of parties made it successful beyond expectation, and its success introduced or confirmed the use of dialogue too declamatory or of unaffecting eloquence and chill philosophy.

Notwithstanding its former success, there can be no doubt it would be entirely unsuitable to the taste of the present day. "It is rather a poem in dialogue than a drama, rather a succession of just sentiments than a representation of natural affections, or of any state probable or possible in human life. Nothing here excites or assuages emotion, here is no magical power of raising fantastic terror or wild anxiety. The events are expected without solicitude, and are remembered without joy or sorrow; we consider not what they are doing or what they are suffering; we wish only to know what they have to say. 'Cato' is a being above our solicitude. For the rest there is not one amongst them that strongly attracts either affection or esteem. But they are made the vehicles of such sentiments and such expressions that there is scarcely a scene in the play which the reader does not wish to impress upon his memory." So writes the surly lexicographer, and I heartily endorse his sentiments.

Dennis was bitterly severe in his remarks upon "Cato;" there was, however, as Dryden expresses it, perhaps "too much horse-play in his raillery." But, if his jests were coarse, his arguments were strong. Yet as all love better to be pleased than to be taught, the tragedy was read, was acted with the greatest applause, and the critic was neglected. Flushed with consciousness of the detections of absurdity in the conduct, Dennis afterwards attacked the sentiments of "Cato;" he then amused himself with petty cavils and minor objections.

Addison's first composition, the opera of "Rosamond," has long since been laid on the shelf; no attempt has ever been made to resuscitate it. The subject is well chosen, the fiction is pleasing, the thoughts are sometimes great and sometimes tender, the versification is easy and gay; but, notwithstanding all the above qualities, it never took hold of the public.

I have a faint idea that I once saw Thomson's "Tancred and Sigismunda" acted, but it left no impression upon my mind. According to the critics of the day, it was the most successful of all his tragedies, and for many years kept its place on the stage. In 1727 Thomson produced another tragedy, entitled "Sophonisba," which met with little success. How often does one unfortunate line lead to the condemnation of a play! Such was the case with the above-mentioned tragedy. The hero has to exclaim,

"Oh, Sophonisba! Sophonisba, oh!"

when a wag thus irreverently parodied the line:

"Oh, Jemmy Thomson! Jemmy Thomson, oh!"

"Agamemnon" was received with little favour. "Edward and Eleonora" was rejected by the licencer of plays. Thomson left behind him the tragedy of "Coriolanus," which, through the zeal of his patron, Sir George Lyttleton, was acted for the benefit of the author's family. It was said by the above-mentioned patron, in the prologue of Thomson's posthumous play, that his works contained

"No line which, dying, he could wish to blot!"

As a dramatic writer Thomson's fame would have never been perpetuated; as the author of

"The Seasons" he raised for himself an imperishable monument.

Richard Cumberland was the author of many comedies, two of which, in my earlier days, were constantly acted, both at the winter theatres in the metropolis and in the provinces. At his father's palace of Clonfort, in Ireland, he composed his drama entitled "The West Indian," and, since he was celebrated as a writer for the stage, it may not be amiss to introduce in this place the generous sentiments with which he was animated in the composition of this and other comedies.

"When I began," he tells us in his memoirs, "to write for the stage, my ambition was to aim at writing something that might be lasting, and outlive me. When temporary subjects were suggested to me I declined them. I formed to myself an idea which I conceived to be the character of a legitimate comedy, and that alone was my object; and, though I did not quite aspire to attain, I was not altogether in despair of approaching it. I perceived that I had fallen upon a time when great eccentricity of character was pretty much gone by; but still I fancied there was an opening for some originality, and an opportunity of showing at least my good will to mankind, if I introduced the characters of persons who had usually been exhibited on the stage as the butts for ridicule and abuse, and endeavoured to present them in such lights as might tend to reconcile the world to them and them to the world. I therefore looked into society for the purpose of discovering such as were the victims of its national, professional, or religious prejudices; in short, for those suffering characters which stood in need of an advocate, and out of these I meditated to select and form heroes for my future dramas, of whom I would study to make such favourable and reconciliatory delineations as might induce the spectators to look upon them with pity, and receive them into their good opinion and esteem."

His "Jew," produced on the stage many years afterwards, is also formed on the principle of combating national and religious prejudices.

The career of Holcroft as a stable-boy, a schoolmaster, a newspaper writer, an actor, and a dramatist, deserves a place among plays and players. He was the son of a shoemaker, and was born in London in 1745. So slender were his father's means that his mother was necessitated to eke out their existence by selling greens, oysters, &c. When the boy was about seven years of age his parents set off on a tramping expedition as pedlars, taking their son with them, but their earnings were so meagre and precarious that the boy had to beg from door to door.

When in his eleventh year the lad commenced life as a stable-boy in a racing stables at Newmarket. Whilst in this employment, as he was one day passing a church, he stopped to listen to the singing. Having mustered courage to enter, he found the choir engaged in the practice of part singing. Being immediately seized with a strong desire to learn the art which had struck him with so much admiration, he sought the acquaintance of the teacher, who, finding Holcroft had a good voice, admitted him into the class, where he applied himself to the study of music with such ardour that he soon acquired a mastery of the science.

Still pursuing his occupation at the stables, he attended most sedulously to his self-education, learning the French language, as also arithmetic—his calculations being worked out on the paling of the stable-yard. What a fortune he might have made in these days as a book-maker! A cute lad, knowing the secrets of the stable, and fully competent to calculate the odds, would prove a formidable rival to the betting men at Tattersal's.

To resume. After leaving Newmarket, young Thomas Holcroft joined his father, who had resumed the trade of shoemaker, and became a skilful workman. During the whole of this time his love of books and study never forsook him. After an attempt to earn a living as a schoolmaster, in which he met with so little success that he was compelled for three months to subsist upon potatoes and butter-milk, he succeeded in becoming a writer for the newspapers.

He next followed the career of an actor, having, it is said, first imbibed a passion for the stage by listening to an itinerant Merry Andrew at Wisbeach Fair. He subsequently produced several original plays, also translating many French works, which he adapted to the English stage. A few months before he died he commenced a memoir of his life, but only succeeded in getting as far as his fifteenth year, when he was laid prostrate by sickness.

"I do not care what severity of treatment you subject me to," he said to his physician, "provided I can live six months to complete my work."

But this was not permitted him, for death intervened, and what would doubtless have proved a most interesting autobiography was left incomplete.

The dramatic literature of the early part of the reign of the third George is very voluminous, consisting principally of comedies and farces. Home, the author of "Douglas," which came out in 1757, followed that first successful effort by about half a dozen attempts in the same style, the last of which, entitled "Alfred," was produced in 1778, but they were all failures. Horace Walpole's tragedy, "The Mysterious Mother," was never acted; it was privately printed in 1768, and many years afterwards it was published.

The principal successful writers at the above period were Goldsmith, Garrick, and Foote, who all died in the earlier part of the reign of George III., and Macklin, Murphy, Cumberland, Colman, Mrs. Cowley, and Sheridan, who mostly survived till after the commencement of the present century.

Goldsmith's admirable comedies of "The Good-natured Man" and "She Stoops to Conquer" were brought out, the former in 1768, the latter in 1773. But the most brilliant contributions made to the dramatic literature of the country were Sheridan's celebrated comedies of "The Rivals," brought out in 1775, when the author was only in his twenty-fifth year, followed the same year by " The Duenna," and " The School for Scandal," which crowned the reputation of one who has been happily called the modern Congreve.

This *chef-d'œuvre* of Sheridan's was brought out in 1776. There can be no doubt that Sheridan's plays bear a favourable comparison with those of Congreve, Vanbrugh, and Farquhar. Sheridan's wit was as polished, if not as quick and dazzling, as Congreve's, and he possessed all the ease and gaiety of Farquhar. His other dramatic pieces are "The Trip to Scarborough," " The Critic," &c., all of which were produced before the year 1780.

CHAPTER X.

FRENCH THEATRICALS—THE TWO HUNDREDTH ANNIVERSARY OF THE COMÉDIE FRANÇAISE—REFORM IN THE COSTUME OF THE ARTISTS.

> The world's a theatre, the earth a stage.
> THOMAS HEYWOOD, 1649.

I NOW turn to the French stage. Wednesday, the 25th of last August, was the two hundredth anniversary of the birth of the Comédie Française, and it may not be out of place to give a slight sketch of its rise and progress.

In 1673, upon the death of Molière, the company he had brought together at the Palais Royal broke up into two bodies; one allied itself to the rivals at the Hôtel de Bourgogne, and the other, headed by his widow, took a theatre which the Marquis de Sourdène had fitted up in the Rue Mazarin for amateur performances.

A violent competition at once set up between the rival houses, which, if it did them no benefit, was of advantage to authors, and in 1680 the King insisted upon their uniting with each other, selecting for their use the theatre that had been occupied in 1673. The company was to consist of twenty-seven persons, and the profits it was decreed should be divided among them according to circumstances; those who wished and had leave to withdraw were to be allowed a pension, and vacancies, as they arose, were to be filled up as the First Gentleman of the Chamber should decide. No other players were permitted to give a French tragedy or comedy in the city or faubourgs of Paris without the consent of the King, and His Majesty granted to the company an annual subsidy of twelve thousand livres payable every six months.

Four years afterwards, owing to the complaints of the scholars at the Collége Mazarin of the annoyance they experienced from the crowds of play-goers, the company removed to a building in the Rue des Fossés St. Germain des Près, and from that time the theatre was known officially as the Comédie Française, but the date of the existence of the institution was as above stated.

The motives that prompted this step on the part of Louis XIV. were not, as might be supposed, those derived from an attachment to literature and art. He had noticed the growing development of the power of the stage, which may be said to have begun when Corneille devoted himself to tragedy, and to have continued with rapid strides through the genius of Molière and Racine. The art of acting increased in proportion to the quality of the material it had to work upon, and from the same period may be dated the improvement in the status of the actor, although he still remained an object of persecution by the Church.

In consequence of the general advance it had made, the stage attracted nearly the whole of the poetical genius of the country, and became the most popular of amusements. Louis had noticed how a play, "Les Précieuses Ridicules," had influenced the tone of French society, and, rightly thinking the same power might be exercised for the purpose of educating the people into sedition, sought by the establishment of the Comédie Française to make the drama subservient to the interests of absolutism.

A performance at the period in question was a very different affair from what it is at the present day. The doors were opened between three and four o'clock, and the theatre, lighted by candles, quickly filled, the select portions of the house being devoted to the gorgeously attired ladies and gentlemen of the *haut monde*, and the pit, unprovided with seats, to the *bourgeoisie*, and others of a similar class, while still another part was reserved for the servants and attendants upon the distinguished portion of the audience. Three raps, as now, announced the rising of the curtain, and the play began.

The actors represented their parts conscientiously, and with the perfection of elocution, and as a poetic study the thing was complete. But of illusion there was none. The heroes of ancient history or fiction wore court suits, and the heroines appeared in a hoop and powdered periwig. There was no scenery, but each side of the stage was occupied by a certain number of exquisites, arrayed in the embroidery and lace of the period, who frequently interrupted the proceedings by walking across the stage to communicate with friends on the opposite side, or to attract the flagging attention of their admirers, who were perhaps devoting a little seriousness to the play. Another source of interruption was the frequent excursions of the servants to snuff the candles, without reference to the importance of the scene in progress. At about nine o'clock the performance was over, and the spectators dispersed to their homes, or other places, for the enjoyment of those famous suppers which played so important a part in the evening's entertainment.

Louis XIV. died, and shortly afterwards Voltaire appeared upon the scene, and, although inferior to his gifted predecessors as a dramatic poet, his works kept the stage for a considerable time, and found interpreters in some of the most distinguished members the society ever possessed. Progress was also made in the representation by the introduction of scenery and appropriate costumes, which also had the effect of banishing the exquisites from the stage, who, while vigorously defending their privileges, could not be blind to the absurdity of a modern Court dress lounging in the palaces and streets of ancient Greece or Rome. Other innovations began to creep in, in the shape of an attempt to introduce domestic drama; and scenes from more modern history than the tragedies of Racine depicted were received with unqualified applause.

Revolution was however at hand. The people had awoke to the sense of the tyranny under which they lived, and their loyalty changed into undisguised detestation. Naturally enough this change in the public mind was forcibly shown in the theatre, and any play that attacked the established order of things was assured of success. In the storm which broke in 1789 the fortunes of the theatre came nearly to an end. Like other communities, the company was torn by political dissensions, and eventually divided into Royalists and Republicans, the former remaining where they were, and the latter, headed by Talma, seeking other quarters. The Royalists were nearly being obliterated by the summary method prevailing at the time, but were saved at some risk by a friend in office, after their death-warrant had been signed.

When the storm had passed over the Comédie Française reunited, and, with varied fortunes, has continued until now. Plays of the classical school are still presented on the boards, but the greater attractions of the romantic have quite superseded them in the national taste, and what the genius of Rachel failed permanently to restore seems a hopeless task for others to try.

Its more recent history is too well known to need comment; enough to say that it holds an acknowledged superiority in theatrical art.

CHAPTER XI.

THE FRENCH STAGE—JODELLE—LA HARPE—HIS CHEQUERED CAREER—HIS TRAGEDIES—"THE EARL OF WARWICK"—"MELANIE"—"BARMECIDES"—"JOAN OF NAPLES"—"MENZIKOFF."

Le théâtre instruit mieux que ne fait un gros livre.
VOLTAIRE.

IT is curious to observe that the first dramatic compositions in France, which succeeded the Mysteries imported by the Pilgrims from the East, were imitations from the Greek tragedies given by Jodelle in 1550, as will be seen by the following extract from the works of an able French historian:—

"Ce fut Jodelle qui, en 1550, osa le premier,

en France, faire jouer une tragédie de son invention; elle était intitulée, 'Cléopâtre Captive.' Apres lui vinrent Robert Garnier, Alexandre Hardi, et Rotrou; mais le Théâtre Français ne prit naissance que sous Pierre Corneille. Ce génie sublime franchit, presque tout-à-coup les espaces immenses qu'il y avait entre les essais informes de son siècle et les productions les plus accomplies de l'art. Lorsque Corneille, commençant à vieillir, cessa de nous transporter d'admiration, Racine vint, qui fit couler des larmes délicieuses; ensuite on vit Crébillon dont le pinceau mâle et sombre nous attendrit et nous épouvante. Enfin parut Voltaire, qui a réuni tous les genres, le tendre, le touchant, le terrible, le grand, et le sublime."

I pass from the year 1550 to the days of La Harpe, who may be ranked among dramatic authors, though perhaps not so successful in that department of literature as in that of journalism. The rank which was so justly assigned to M. La Harpe among the literati of France, and his various works (many of them possessing high utility and value) entitle him to special notice, and fully justify our quoting from his most valuable remarks on the drama, and giving a brief sketch of his life.

Jean François De La Harpe was born in Paris in 1740. Though his family was noble, he was left a helpless orphan, and owed his education to the compassion of a few pious persons, who placed him in one of those institutions for the relief of such subjects, with which Paris at that time abounded. The same benevolent individuals afterwards obtained his admission into the University on a charitable foundation. His existence depended in a manner on his success; and the colleges, it is remarked, owed their celebrity principally to young men in this predicament, since it rarely happened that, thus destitute of friends, and depending on their efforts alone, they failed to distinguish themselves by their talents or their industry.

La Harpe, however, in the more early stages of his academic course, gave no promise of the great parts which he afterwards displayed.

He could not struggle with that which he could not understand, and his fine talents disdained the drudgery of treasuring up mere words; but, when he reached the higher classes, his excellent understanding and his exquisite imagination placed him in the foremost rank, and for two years he gained all the prizes, a degree of success which was without example.

The academic triumphs of the young collegian were reported in the circles of society; he was made the topic of conversation, and it became so much the fashion to have him to parties that he was known in the world before he had finished his studies. This flattering notice did not intoxicate him, for he continued his pursuits, and did not rest satisfied with his college achievements.

In referring to La Harpe's works I shall confine myself to those connected with the drama. When twenty-two years old he presented to the theatre his very successful tragedy "The Earl of Warwick." The failure of his next dramatic performance plunged La Harpe, who was now married, into those difficulties with which it is so generally the fate of literary men to struggle. In this situation the doors of Ferney were thrown open to him, and the young couple became the guests of Voltaire during thirteen months. His good offices with the Duc de Choiseul, and further attempts at the drama were, however, ineffectual, and the youthful aspirant was obliged to depend on exertions of another kind. Lacombe engaged him to write in the *Mercure*.

This journal, the sole merits of which had been that of favouring the opinions then in vogue, being placed under the direction of La Harpe, soon exhibited a new aspect. Sound criticism, humorous discussion, and profound and comprehensive views supplied the place of the shallow declamations with which it had till that time been filled. Though he continued his labours in the *Mercure*, he did not neglect the theatre, and his "Melanie" met with considerable success. In his "Barmécides" he delineates the generous mind, and "Joan of Naples" exemplifies the mischievous consequences of the passions, while in "Menzikoff" we witness the fall of a powerful minister, accompanied with resignation which is unexampled.

CHAPTER XII.

THE PERFECTION OF TRAGEDY DESCRIBED BY ARISTOTLE—LA HARPE'S CRITICISMS—CORNEILLE—VOLTAIRE—PENSIONS GRANTED BY LOUIS XIV. TO MEN OF SCIENCE AND LITERATURE—M. CAPELLE REMARKS ON SHAKESPEARE AND ADDISON—AKENSIDE ON THE GENIUS OF SHAKESPEARE.

La tragédie, informe et grossière en naissant,
N'etait qu'un simple chœur où chacun, en dansant,
Et du dieu des raisins entonnant les louanges,
S'efforçait d'attirer des fertiles vendanges.
Là, le vin et la joie éveillant les esprits,
Du plus habile chantre un bouc était le prix,
Thespis fut le premier qui, barbouillé de lie,
Promène per les bourgs cette heureuse folie,
Et d'acteurs mal ornés cherzeant un tomberau,
Amusa les passans d'un spectacle nouveau.
Eschyle dans le chœur jeta les personnages ;
D'un masque plus honnête habilla les visages
Sur les ais d'un théâtre en public exhaussé,
Fit paraître l'acteur d'un brodequin chaussé.

> Sophocle enfin, donnant l'essor à son génie,
> Accrut encor la pompe, augmenta l'harmonie,
> Intéressa la chœur dans fonte l'action,
> Des vers trop raboteux polit expression ;
> Lui donna chez les Grecs cette hauteur divine,
> On jamais n'atteignit la faiblesse latine.
>
> BOÏLEAU.

"IT is required," by Aristotle, "to the perfection of a tragedy, and is equally necessary in every other species of regular composition, that it should have a beginning, a middle, and an end. The beginning," says this great critic, "is that which has nothing necessarily previous, but to which that which follows is naturally consequent; the end, on the contrary, is that which by necessity, or at least according to the common course of things, succeeds something else, but which implies nothing consequent to itself; the middle is connected on one side with something that naturally goes before, and on the other with something that naturally follows it."

Such is the rule laid down by Aristotle for the disposition of the different parts of a well-constituted fable. It must begin where it may be made intelligible without introduction; and end where the mind is left in repose, without expectation of any further event. The intermediate passages must join the last effect to the first cause by a regular and unbroken concatenation; nothing must be therefore inserted which does not apparently arise from something foregoing, and properly make way for something that succeeds it. The above remarks were written a hundred and thirty years ago.

Jean François La Harpe tells us that nothing is more common than to find well-informed persons declaring that the ancient Greek dramas are superior to more modern ones, and they quote Æschylus, Sophocles, and Euripedes, who they consider never were surpassed, and never can be surpassed. He proceeds to account for this by saying:

"There are always among the learned a class of men who admire nothing but the ancients, because they cherish exclusively the objects of their study, and who cannot or will not translate the moderns. On the other hand, there are men of unquestionable talent who have paid little attention to the study of antiquity, or who cannot accustom themselves to manners so different from those of their own country, who look upon Greek tragedy as nothing but dramatic declamation, and do not see the infancy of the art which has been brought to perfection."

Both the above opinions the celebrated French critic considers unjust; he then proceeds to notice the works of Corneille, Racine, and Voltaire, which he justly commends.

La Harpe then proceeds to notice French comedy previous to the time of Molière, the introduction of which he attributes to Italy and Spain.

Of Molière he says :—

"L'eloge d'un écrivain est dans ses ouvrages."—Many men of undoubted talent and pungent wit have appeared after him, without, however, approaching him. Some have possessed much gaiety, others have produced clever verses, and many have faithfully depicted manners.—" Mais le peinture de l'esprit humain à été l'art de Molière; c'est la carrière qu'il a ouverte et qu'il a fermée; il n'y a rien en ce genre, ni avant lui, ni après."

I should take away the spirit of the above if I attempted to translate it.

Corneille's principal works are "Médée," "Le Cid," "Horace," "Cinna," "Polyeucte," "Pompée," "Rodogune," "Heraclius," "Nicomède," "Sartorius," "Théodore," and "Attila." "Médée" was the dramatist's first production; the selection of the subject not being a happy one, the tragedy produced no great effect. "Le Cid," founded on Spanish literature, then much in vogue in France, followed, and proved the glory of the French stage; then came "Horace," adding much to the dramatic fame of the author. "Cinna," which came next after "Horace," was pronounced to be a grand success. "Polyeucte" was spoken highly of by the critics. "Pompée" was replete with beautiful verse. In "Rodogune" there were some splendid, truly terrific scenes, notably that when Cleopatra, before preparing the poison for her son and Rodogune, hopes to live long enough to see them die before her. "Heraclius" was founded on Spanish history, and was not approved of, nor were the rest of his works.

Racine was the author of "Les Frères Ennemis," "Alexandre," "Britannicus," "Bérénice," "Bajazet," "Mithridate," "Iphigénie, "Phèdre," "Esther," and "Athalie."

"Les Frères Ennemis" met with tolerable success, the hatred of the two brothers being carried out with vindictive bitterness; still the subject was repulsive.

I have already said that "Le Cid" was the first glory of the French stage, its most brilliant epoch, and "Andromaque" was the second, and produced quite as great a *furore*. In Corneille's drama the author was partly indebted to the Spanish writer, in Racine's the author had no such assistance.

"Britannicus," though censured by the critics, kept possession of the stage for many long years. In "Bérénice" Racine was fully aware of the difficulties of the subject, that of producing a successful tragedy from an heroic elegy; still he conquered that difficulty, and "Bérénice" was a success. "Bajazet" was a work of the author's choice, and fully justified his selection of it. In "Mithridate" Racine seemed desirous of following Corneille by placing on the scene one of those splendid characters of antiquity, which laid him open to the censure of the friends of the former. The tragedy, however, was replete with fine writing and dramatic situations. "Iphigénie" is unquestionably the master-piece of Euripedes, and Racine, in adapting the subject, did not fail to express the advantages he had received from the perusal of the original work.

"Phèdre" created a great sensation during a period of six weeks, but at the end of the year, when about to be revived, through the "wild vicissitudes of taste," the subject being forgotten, the idea was abandoned. Many a less effective piece found favour with the public. "Esther" met with great success at St. Cyr, but was never brought forward on the regular stage until after the death of the author.

Following the ancient usage, Racine introduced choruses both in "Esther" and "Athalie," which proved highly effective.

Voltaire was the author of " Œdipe," "Mariamne," "Brutus," "Zaïre," "Adelaide," "La Mort de Cæsar," "Alzire," "Zulime," "Mahomet," "Merope," "Semiramis," "Rome Sauvée," "L'Orphelin de la Chine," "Tancrède," "Olympie," and other pieces, written later in life.

When "Œdipe" was first produced, the critics declared the author to be a worthy successor of Corneille, and so he proved to be. When "Mariamne" was brought out, Voltaire had to contend against that difficulty to which all writers are subjected, namely, to produce a second piece equal to the first. Expectation is always alive upon such occasions, and the illiberal are apt to indulge in comparisons as to the respective merits of the pieces. The general opinion was that "Mariamne" was not equal to "Œdipe."

"Brutus" was loudly applauded, and greatly

admired by connoisseurs, but not much sought after by the public. "Zaïre" brought tears into the eyes of many. What greater praise can be given to a tragedy? "Adelaïde" was pronounced to be inferior to "Zaïre." "La Mort de Cæsar" was brilliant in language and situations. "Alzire" was rather severely criticised, and many of the reasons assigned for so unfavourable a notice were not without justice. In "Zulime" and "Mahomet" the versification was very weak, nor were the characters well delineated.

For more than two thousand years "Merope" was a subject well worthy of a tragic writer, as one of the noblest works of Aristotle; and Voltaire did ample justice to "Semiramis."

Voltaire could not have done more honour to Sophocles than in imitating him—nay more, in some respects surpassing him. Notwithstanding this, "Oreste," when first produced, was worse treated than "Semiramis."

"Rome Sauvée" was never very popular on the French stage. "L'Orphelin de la Chine" proved a great success. Nothing can exceed the fierce agony and exquisite pathos in the second act, when Idame appeals to Zamti to save her son:—

IDAME:

Qu'ai-je-vu ? Qu'a-t-on fait ? Barbare, est il possible ?
L'avez-vous commandé, ce sacrifice horrible ?
Non, je ne puis le croire, et le ciel irrité.
N'a pas dans votre sein mis tant de cruauté,
Non, vous ne serez point plus dur et plus barbare
Que la loi du vainqueur et le fer du Tartare.
Vous pleurez, malheureux !

ZAMTI:

    Ah ! pleurez avec moi
Mais avec moi songez à sauver votre roi.

IDAME:

Que j'immole mon fils !

ZAMTI:

    Telle est notre misère ;
Vous etez citoyenne avant que d'etre mère.

IDAME:

Quoi ! sur toi la nature a si peu de pouvoir.

ZAMTI:

Elle n'en a que trop, mais moins que mon devoir,
Et je dois plus au sang de mon malheureux maître
Qu'a cet enfant obscur à qui j'ai donné l'être.

Then follows Idame's denunciation of her husband's "horrible virtue," succeeded by a true touch of nature from Zamti, which is but momentary, for he again refers to his devotion to the king. This calls for a more vehement protest from the unhappy mother. A finer scene was never represented on the stage, and the *dénouement* of the tragedy is truly dramatic.

An adventure between Ariodant and Genèvre in a poem of Ariosto, afterwards introduced into a romance of Madame de Fontaine's, entitled "La Comtesse de Savoie," furnished Voltaire a subject for "Tancrède," which he adapted in his sixty-fourth year, and showed some traces of weakness in its composition. The same remark applies to "Olympie" and "Le Triumvirat."

Crébillon was the author of "Idomenée," "Altrée et Thyeste," "Rhadamiste,"—which was unquestionably the best of his pieces—"Xerxes," "Semiramis," "Pyrrhus," "Catiline," and others.

In summing up the dramatists whose works

I have recorded, I may remark that Corneille was famed for his sublime conceptions, Racine for his thorough knowledge of human nature, Voltaire for his word-painting of manners and dramatic effects. Many, however, who have attentively perused Crébillon's works will place him third, or at least fourth, on the pedestal of fame devoted to tragedy. La Grange Chancel, La Motte Pirot, Le Franc de Pompignan were also famed for their tragedies.

A list of the men of science and letters, both French and foreigners, whom Louis XIV. pensioned, together with the sums assigned to each, appears in the life of this monarch. It is taken from the MSS. of Colbert, and the measure was adopted in 1663. In this account the great Corneille is styled the first dramatic poet in the world, and the sum of two thousand livres stands opposite his name; some other literati have as much as four thousand, while the exquisite Racine has only eight hundred.

"L'Angleterre a produit un petit nombre d'auteurs tragiques, parmi lesquels on distingue

Shakespeare, qui offre des étincelles de génie, mais brut et inculte ; et Addison, qui est plus correct et plus astreint aux règles dramatiques."

So writes M. Capelle in his " Dictionnaire de Morale, de Science, et de Littérature, ou Choix de Pensées Ingénieuses et Sublimes, de Dissertations et de Definitions ; extraites des plus célèbres Moralistes, Orateurs, Poëtes, et Savants. Pour servir de délassement aux Etudes, former le cœur, et mouvoir la mémoire des jeunes gens."

The motto of the book runs as follows:—
"Heureux qui peut mêler l'agréable à l'utile;" but in the comparison between Shakespeare and Addison, however *agreeable* it may be for M. Capelle to underrate our greatest bard, it certainly does not add to the *utility* of the work. We are indeed astounded that an author of M. Capelle's capabilities should have fallen into such an error. Let us turn to another writer, Akenside, whose opinion we value more than that of the French critic.

How beautifully has our poet described the

genius of that mighty spirit, that Proteus of the drama, who changes himself into each character, and enters into every condition of human nature.

> "O, youths and virgins! O, declining old!
> O, pale misfortune's slaves! O, ye who dwell
> Unknown, with humble quiet! Ye who wait
> In courts, and fill the golden seat of kings!
> O, sons of sport and pleasure! O, thou wretch
> That weep'st for jealous love, and the sore wound
> Of conscious guilt, or death's rapacious hand,
> That left thee void of hope! O, ye who mourn
> In exile! Ye who through the embattled field
> Seek bright renown; or who for nobler palms
> Contend, the leaders of a public cause;
> Hath not his faithful tongue
> Told you the fashion of your own estate,
> The secrets of your bosom?"

Byron's remarks, too, applied to one of his distinguished predecessors, are so applicable to the immortal bard that I cannot resist quoting them.

"Neither time, nor distance, nor grief, nor age can ever diminish our veneration for him who is the great poet of all times, of all climes, of all feelings, and of all stages of existence. The delight of our boyhood, the study of our manhood, perhaps—if allowed to us to attain it—the consolation of our age. He has assembled all that a good and great man can gather together of wisdom, clothed in consummate beauty."

CHAPTER XIII.

FRENCH COMEDY—MOLIÈRE—LE SAGE—QUIRAULT—BRUEYS—REGNARD—DANCOURT—SAINT FOIX—DIDEROT—SEDAINE—DESTOUCHES—BOÏSSY—FABRE D'EGLANTINE.

To hold, as 'twere, the mirror up to nature, to show virtue her own feature, scorn her own image, and the very age and body of the time his form and pressure.
SHAKESPEARE.

ROUSSEAU is very severe in his remarks upon the drama, for he writes:—" Le théâtre qui ne peut rien pour corriger les mœurs, peut beaucoup pour les altérer," which is almost as illiberal as De Bonald's comments on comedy in his " Pensées Diverses," who says: —" La comédie corrige les manières et le théâtre corrompe les mœurs."

I now turn to Molière, who was the creator of the French comedy, and, it may be said, the founder of a national theatre. It was as a strolling leader of a small itinerant band, rambling from province to province, that he composed and acted his "Etourdi," his "Dépit Amoureux," his inimitable "Précieuses Ridicules," his "Médicin Malgré Lui," and many others of his best comedies. His *début* in Paris was a complete failure, and it was not until after many struggles that his genius was recognized.

On his arrival at Paris in 1635 he played at the sign of "La Croix Blanche," in the Faubourg St. Germain, and did not receive his patent from the King for his theatre in the Palais Royal until the year 1660.

During a very lengthened career I have seen, in England and France, the most interesting, the best acted pieces in tragedy, comedy, opera, and farce, but I never witnessed any with greater delight than I did Molière's "Tartuffe," at the Théâtre Français. Mademoiselle Mars as Eloire was inimitable.

Among other artists connected with the above theatre, Michaud and Fleury must not be passed over. Michaud's acting was unrivalled, and his pure, genuine, and truly comic humour was entirely free from grimace or over-charging. Fleury, in a higher range of parts, if less broadly amusing, was not less excellent and eminent.

Le Sage, who was devoted to Spanish literature, gained more celebrity by his romances than his dramatic works. "Gil Blas" will remain an imperishable monument of his talent as a writer of prose. "Turcuret" was a great success. Among his lighter pieces may be mentioned "Crispin Rival de son Maître," "Les Carrosses d'Orléans," "Le Charivari," and "Colin Maillard," many of which held possession of the stage long after the death of the author.

Le Grand was a prolific writer. Among his best works are "Le Procureur Arbitre" and "L'Impromptu de Campagne." In addition to the above, to suit the taste of the time, he produced ballets and spectacles, the latter of which included " Le Roi de Cosaque," " Les Amazones Modernes," " Le Nouveauté," and " Le Triomphe du Temps."

Fagan came next, and trod in the track of Le Grand, producing " Le Rendezvous " and " La Pupille," which had an extraordinary long run.

Among the best light pieces of the day I write of was " Le Magnifique," by La Motte; " L'Anglomanie " and " Les Mœurs du Temps," by Sauvin ; " Le Complaisant," by Pont-de-Veyle ; " L'Impertinent," by Desmatris ; " Les Fausses Infidelités," by Barthe. Collé was the author of two successful pieces, " Dupuis et Desronnis " and " La Partie de Chasse," the latter founded on an English piece. " Dupuis et Desronnis " was adapted from a French romance.

La Noue was a popular actor, highly respected in his profession, and took a part in his most successful piece, " La Coquette Corrigée." Like many other plays, it produced little effect on its first representation, but finally proved highly attractive. Marivaux's pieces, " La

Surprise de l'Amour," "L'Epreuve," "Le Préjugé Vaincu," proved successful. Saint Foix wrote a few trifling pieces, which were unworthy the name of comedies. Chamfort, among other dramatic works, wrote a remarkably interesting play, entitled "La Jeune Indienne." He was also the author of "Le Marchand de Smyrne."

La Chaussée merits a larger space than I can in this *precis* history afford him. He was a most prolific writer, and, among other pieces, produced "Préjugé à la Mode," "L'Ecole des Amis," "L'Homme de Fortune," and "Amour pour Amour." Perhaps the most successful one was "L'Ecole des Mères."

La Harpe tells us that Voltaire failed as a writer of comedy, but he praises his drama of "Nanine," which, though less successful than his "Enfant Prodigue," was, he considered, a more interesting piece. Diderot devoted his talents to serious and domestic dramas. His first dramatic production was entitled "Le Fils Naturel," which caused a perfect furore. His "Père de Famille" was also for a length of time a favourite on the French stage; albeit, according to the verdict of a celebrated critic, it hardly merited that success, for he remarks: "This piece is a series of exclamations, of invocations, of lamentations. The father of the family weeps, St. Albin weeps, Sophia weeps, and Cécile weeps."

Sauvin's most popular piece was "Beverley," taken from Lillo's tragedy of "The Gamester." Sedaine produced a drama entitled "Le Philosophe sans le Savoir," originally called "Le Duel," a title objected to by the licenser. His "Gageure Imprévue," founded on a story of Scarron's, was an original and amusing piece.

La Harpe then introduces what he terms an inferior order of writers, commencing with Quirault, who, in 1665, produced a comedy entitled "Les Amants Brouillés." After a lovers' quarrel, caused by a false report, between Isabelle and Acante, the former, wishing for an *éclaircissement*, writes as follows:—

"Je voudrais vous parler, et nous voir seuls tous deux,
Je ne conçois pas bien pourquoi je le désire!

> Je ne sais ce que je vous veux ;
> Mais n'auriez-vous rien a me dire ?"

Brueys produced "L'Avocat Patelin," "Le Grondeur," &c. Campistron in "Le Jaloux Désabusé," proved that his talents were better suited for comedy than tragedy. Baron produced a piece founded on Terence's "Andria." In 1696 Regnard produced "Le Joueur," a comedy in five acts, who, though not a rival, was looked upon as a worthy successor to Molière. "Le Legataire," next in merit to "Le Joueur," after a time followed, but it was censured as not conveying a good moral. "Les Ménechmes," taken from Plautus, proved highly amusing and attractive, as did some other comedies from the same writer.

Dubresny produced "Le Chevalier Joueur," "La Noce Interrompue," "La Joueuse," "La Maladie sans Maladie," "Le Faux Honnette Homme," and "Le Jaloux Honteux," the majority of which produced no effect, or, as the critic remarks, "sank never to rise again." Dancourt wrote successfully "Le Galant Jardinier," "Le

Mari Retrouvé," "Les Trois Cousines," and "Les Bourgeoises de Qualité." He was less successful in "Point de Bezons," "La Foire de St. Germain," "La Déroute du Phanon," "La Désolation des Joueuses," "L'Operateur Barry," "Le Vert-Galant," "Le Retour des Officiers," "Les Eaux de Bourbon," "Les Fêtes du Cours," and "Les Agioteurs."

From Dancourt to Hautéroche the descent is great. His "Esprit Follet," an Italian drama in the style of Scarron, amused the multitude. "Crispin Medecin" and "Le Cocher Supposé" owed their success to the indulgence of the public.

I now approach the XVIII. Siècle, when Destouches must take precedence, not as regards merit, quantity, not quality, being his characteristic. He was the author of the "Curieux Impertinent," "L'Ingrat," "Le Philosophe Amoureux," "L'Obstacle Imprevu," "L'Ambiteux," "Le Medisant," "L'Enfant Gâté," "L'Aimable Vieillard," "L'Amour Usé," "L'Homme Singulier," "La Force du Naturel,"

"Jeune Homme à L'Epreuvé," "Trésor Caché," "Dépôt," "Le Mari Confident," and "L'Archimenteur."

In enumerating the above titles, one is disposed to say with Chicaneau:

"Si j'en counais pas un, je veux être étranglé."

What perhaps is better is not to know any. Throughout we have an insipid monotony of intrigues, common-place, cold, or far-fetched; scenes of vapid *plaisanteries;* lovers uttering hackneyed sentiments; glaring imitations of Molière and Regnard. After the death of Destouches some of his other pieces were brought forward. "La Fausse Agnes," "Le Tambour Nocturne," founded on an English comedy, "Le Dissipateur," and others which "ne vaut pas l'honneur d'être nominée."

It is but just to Destouches to say that "Le Philosophe Marié" and "La Glorieux" were thoroughly successful, and deservedly so.

Piron comes next. His "Amant Mystérieux" was acted with "Les Courses de Tempé." One failed, the other met with tolerable success, probably because the audience were more indulgent to the pastoral than to the comedy. Time did them equal justice, for both were buried in oblivion. The author had the courage to avow, in his preface, that "L'Amant Mystérieux" merited its fate. With regard to "Les Courses de Tempé," the piece was unworthy the talent of Piron; it was badly conceived and badly written. "Les Filles Ingrates" was even worse than "L'Ingrat" of Destouches. It is difficult to find a gem among so many false stones; the only one we can select is uttered by a father:—

> "Devais je à votre avis thésaurisant, sans cesse,
> Imiter ces vieillards, tyrans de la jeunesse,
> Qui la faisant languir, sans être plus heureux,
> La privent des plaisirs qui sont perdu pour eux."

Piron also wrote the libretto of the opera "La Metromanie." "Le Mechant," by Gresset, reminds one of "The Flatterer" of Rousseau. The plots of both comedies turn upon a lover anxious to replace his rival by breaking off his marriage. A valet, won over by a waiting maid, unmasks the traitor, and furnishes the real lover with information which foils the scheme of the other. Gresset's plot is better conceived than that of Rousseau, being much more natural.

Few comedies can compare with "Le Mechant," both as regards sound sense, morality, and exquisite verse. It was, however, severely criticised by some detractors, to whom a friend remarked,

"You will probably not have so clever a piece for the next twenty years."

The prophecy was unheeded at the time, but it has been realized, and, at this lapse of time, few French comedies can be compared with "Le Mechant." "Sidney," acted some years previously, did not attain the same success.

Boissy is another author who, like our English single-speech Hamilton, only produced one play that took possession of the stage. He was a prolific writer, two of his works having been resuscitated after the death of the author. He was the author of "L'Epoux par Supercherie," "Le Sage Etourdi," "Le Babillard," and " Le Français à Londres." In the latter we have Milord Houzey and Jacques Rosbif, both characters highly caricatured, " L'Homme du Jour," " Les Dehors Trompeurs."

Fabre d'Eglantine, a provincial actor, came to Paris a short time previous to the Revolution, bringing with him a dozen of plays, including tragedies, comedies, and comic operas. Many of them were not played, and those that were played met with a moderate amount of success.

Beaumarchais was, like his distinguished compatriot, J. J. Rousseau, the son of a watchmaker. Early in life he devoted himself to the study of music; but we must refer our readers to his memoirs, which are deeply interesting, and full of romantic incidents. He was the author of " La Mère Coupable," " Eugénie," " Les Deux Amis," " Parare," " Le Barbier de Seville," and " La Noce de Figaro." Few pieces have proved more deservedly successful than " The Barber of Seville" and the "Marriage of Figaro." They have been acted and sung in almost every civilized language. Rossini's and Mozart's loveliest airs have thus been "married to immortal verse."

CHAPTER XIV.

DUELS OF ACTORS—GEORGE GARRICK, BROTHER TO DAVID GARRICK, AND BADDELEY—J. P. KEMBLE AND AIKIN—ROSELLE AND RIBOU—FLEURY AND DUGAZON—LARIVE AND FLORENCE—TALMA AND NAUDET—ACTRESSES EQUALLY PUGNACIOUS—MESDEMOISELLES BEAUPRÉ AND CATHERINE DES URLIS—MESDEMOISELLES THEODORE AND BEAUMESUIL—MADEMOISELLE MAUPIN'S RENCONTRE WITH M. DUMESNIL—INEBRIETY—MADEMOISELLE LAGUERRE—IPHIGÉNIE EN "CHAMPAGNE," PAS EN AULIDE—OTHER BIBACIOUS ARTISTS—PUFFING ADVERTISEMENTS—REALISTIC STAGE EFFECTS.

> Les hommes, ennemis de leur propre bonheur,
> De la noire Discorde et du faux point d'honneur,
> Ont formé le Duel, dont la main sanguinaire,
> Soutient de leur orgueil la cause imaginaire.
> L'ABBÉ DE VILLIERS.

"WHERE they do agree on the stage, their unanimity is wonderful." So writes

Richard Brinsley Sheridan, in his admirable farce of "The Critic," and it seldom happens that when quarrels occur they lead to extremities.

The only instances of duels between English actors which I can find were the two following. The first took place between George Garrick, brother to David, and Mr. Baddeley, the actor. It was generally reported that George Garrick had induced Mrs. Baddeley to break her matrimonial vow. They fought. Baddeley was so nervous that he could hardly hold his pistol; his antagonist was perfectly cool. When his turn came, he fired in the air, thus ending the affair. At this moment a hackney coach drew up, and out rushed the frail fair one, all beauty and dishevelled hair. Throwing herself on her knees between the combatants, she exclaimed, "Save him! save him!" This was addressed to each in turn; then, falling into her husband's arms, she afterwards rushed into those of her lover.

Another bloodless duel took place on the 1st of March, 1792, between John Philip Kemble and Mr. Aikin—probably some theatrical squabble.

Duels between French actors were much more prevalent, and much more sanguinary than those I have recorded of English *artistes*, Roselli was killed in one of these meetings by Ribou, who belonged to the same dramatic corps. The quarrel arose from the latter declining to give up a favourite part of his to his rival. Roselli, who was of a very conciliatory disposition, and a very indifferent swordsman, wished to avoid the conflict, but Ribou forced it on him. The meeting took place in the street, near Saint Sulpice, at nine o'clock in the evening. Roselli was mortally wounded, and died a few days afterwards. In the generosity of his nature, he did all in his power to screen his murderer from the penalties of the law.

Fleury, another actor, had many encounters with Dugazon. In 1781 Larive and Florence crossed swords on the stage behind the curtain. Many thought they were not in earnest, but, on discovering their mistake, separated them. Another meeting took place the following morning in the Champs Elysées, when Larive thrice disarmed his antagonist without a drop of blood being spilled. In 1790 Talma fought Naudet with pistols, when little harm ensued.

The actresses were quite as pugnacious as their brother actors. Mademoiselle Beaupré sent a challenge to a sister *artiste*, Catherine des Urlis, in consequence of some theatrical or private dispute. They fought with swords in the Palais Royal Theatre. Catherine received a severe wound, and would have fallen a victim to the rage of her rival, had she not made a timely escape. This affair happened in 1649.

In the eighteenth century, Mesdemoiselles Theodore, a celebrated dancer, and Beaumesuil, a singer, both attached to the Opera House, arranged a meeting at the Porte Maillot, in consequence of a jealous quarrel. They went to the appointed spot in their carriages, dressed *en Amazones*, Mademoiselle Theodore taking Mesdemoiselles Fel and Charmoy as her seconds,

Mademoiselle Beaumesuil Mesdemoiselles Geslin and Guomard as hers. As the pistols were about to be presented to the fair combatants, Rey, the thorough bass singer of the same theatre, interfered, and by his eloquence did his best to calm their ruffled feelings, but in vain. They insisted upon the affair proceeding, when Rey, during a final appeal, placed the weapons on the wet grass, and, as they missed fire, nothing was left to the two rivals but to embrace one another.

In 1820 two female dancers fought behind the curtain with blunt foils, but with an ardour that might have led to serious consequences. The quarrel arose regarding a rich Swedish Count, or rather about his dog, the two coryphées disputing as to who should possess its gold collar.

The celebrated Mademoiselle Maupin, who was introduced as the heroine of one of M. Théophile Gautier's romances, was truly pugnacious, and, among other conflicts, once fought three men, and came off victorious. Insulted by Dumesnil, an opera singer, she disguised herself as a man, met her assailant in the Place des Victoires, and, on his refusing to draw his sword, struck him with her cane.

Charges have been brought against English actors of their being addicted to the bottle, and there can be no doubt that in some deeply to be lamented instances such has been the case, but foreign artists are not exempt from the above charge. Mademoiselle Dumesnil owed her inspiration to indulging in wine; between every act she drank largely, and often left the stage to recruit her force with intoxicating draughts. It was owing to this excess that Marmontel attributed the failure of his "Héraclides," in which she played a principal character. An attempt was made to discharge this actress on charges so repugnant to the female sex. Many of Mademoiselle Dumesnil's supporters acquitted her of this charge, declaring that the drams she was accused of taking were chicken broth, flavoured with a little wine.

Another instance is on record where difference of opinion existed as to the inebriety of an actress, namely, in that of Mademoiselle Laguerre of the Opera House. Unfortunately for her, some cruel spectator, upon seeing her in "Iphigénie en Aulide," declared to his neighbour that the title ought to be "*Iphigénie en Champagne!*"

Among actors, Rosimond, Champrueste, Brécourt, Raisir Cadet, La Thorillière fils, Blainville were potent drinkers, but were exceeded by Durneni, a leading operatic artist, who required six bottles of champagne at each representation, in order to give effect to his talent. François Arnould often appeared in a drunken state upon the stage.

Many actresses, though not addicted to drink, have ruined their constitutions by other means. I find that Mademoiselle Contat hastened her death by taking every morning a pint of vinegar in the hope of reducing her fat. Again, we are told of other eccentricities among actresses. Mademoiselle Clairon, in her memoirs, says that in private life, even in her rural retreat to the country, she always kept up the style and dignity of a princess, so as never to appear as an ordinary person, or follow their manners. The same was said of Mademoiselle le Mauve, a celebrated singer.

M. J. Janin recounts, in his "History of Dramatic Literature," that Mademoiselle Sainval seriously considered herself to be always a queen, instead of one on the mimic boards—so much so that she was in the habit, when not playing tragedy, of enveloping herself entirely in a long black veil.

The author of the above story omits to mention whether he refers to the elder or younger Mademoiselle Sainval; probably, however, he alludes to the elder.

Fleury, in his memoirs, recounts the extraordinary and almost incredible pains he took when studying the part of Frederick the Great, in a piece entitled "The Two Pages," so as to keep up the illusion. He first made himself thoroughly acquainted with the manner and conversation of the king, studied his attitudes from his numerous authentic portraits, gave his apartment the name of Potsdam, devoted three months to the most minute details of Frederick's life, and at last brought himself to believe he was the King himself. Every morning he appeared in the uniform, the boots, the hat, the sword, in short the whole costume of the monarch, and showed off his regal powers to those about him. Notwithstanding all these attempts to personify the Frederick, his figure was against him; so, as a last resource, he learnt to play on the flute, thus hoping to acquire the movement of the monarch's head. He gave his servant the name of "Hupar," and his cat that of the dog of the philosophic King.

The above endeavours proved successful, and Fleury's representation of Frederick the Great produced a perfect furore.

The Parisian ballet-girl, with every temptation to drink, happily avoids its intoxicating influence.

While upon the subject of French theatricals, I may remark that puffing advertisements are not confined to England; as the following one, that appeared in a French newspaper, will show. It is dated July, 1833.

"Mademoiselle Georges is now travelling through the departments of France, exhibiting on their boards that rather extravagant mode of performing which is not always relished in the capital. She carries with her a kind of herald of her fame; and this writer, in one of the journals, styles her 'The queen of fine actresses; the most beautiful woman at present on the stage.'"

The following is the circular letter by which the manager of the theatre at Angers invited the chief persons of his district to attend the performances of this "Queen of Beautiful Actresses":—

"MONSIEUR,

"Mademoiselle Georges, the first tragic performer of France, and of the two theatres of the capital, having been pleased to consent to appear on the stage to which I endeavour to draw the honourable public, I dare hope that you will deign to encourage my efforts by a tribute of admiration in favour of the most beautiful woman in Europe—such a woman as has not her equal—in all the pomp of her brilliancy. The pupil of Talma and Mademoiselle Roncourt, and, above all, of beneficent and generous nature. In coming to see Mademoiselle Georges, you will see at once Nature, Talma and Roncourt. In the first part of 'Semiramis' she will appear with one hundred thousand crowns' worth of diamonds; all the ornaments which she wears in that tragedy are precious stones."

The above high-flown language can only be equalled by the eloquence of an American counsel, in defending a popular actress from a slanderous attack in the newspapers. In the middle of an appeal to the jury to mark their abhorrence of the libeller by giving large damages, he delivers the following burst of genius:—

"Slander, gentlemen, like a boa-constrictor of gigantic size and immeasurable proportions, wraps the coils of its unwieldy body about the unfortunate victim, and, heedless of the shrieks of agony that come from the inmost depths of the victim's soul, loud and reverberating as the mighty thunder that rolls in the heavens, it finally breaks its unlucky neck against the iron wheel of public opinion, forcing him to desperation, then to madness, and finally crushing him in the hideous jaws of moral death."

Before I conclude this chapter I must offer a few remarks upon a very hard-worked and ill-paid member of the theatrical profession. I refer to the poor ballet-girl, who has a hard life of it. She must get up before day-break on the cold raw mornings of mid-winter, to take her dancing-lesson; and again at midnight, when the opera is over, she has to find her way on foot, through snow and rain, to her humble lodging at Montmartre or Batignolles. The idea of riding in an omnibus must not enter her head, for while in the lowest rank of her calling she has but a franc a night, even when grown up and promoted to the "second quadrille," she earns only seven hundred francs a year.

Of such stern materials are our entertainments made, and in no department of public amusement is a more rigid economy practised than in the salaries of dancers.

Advancement comes very slowly. It is considered a great thing to move up from the second to the "first quadrille," for then the salary is raised to a thousand francs yearly, being just enough, with frugal management, to keep body and soul together.

From the first quadrille to the second "coryphées" is a still more vigorous step forward, and is rewarded with one thousand three hundred francs a year, or say just twenty francs a week. The next step upward is to the envied position of "premier coryphée," possessing the superb emolument of one thousand five hundred francs a year.

Finally, after years and years of patient study, the dancing-girl attains the summit of her ambition, and rises into a "*petit sujet*," which gives her an individuality before the footlights. This giddy height of glory, and pay amounting to one thousand six hundred francs, or, in exceptional cases, to two thousand francs a year, is the largest reward that dancing genius can expect under ordinary circumstances, for the Eslers and Taglionis form a class apart. Here and no farther can a dancing-girl go, after a blameless youth passed in diligent capers at rehearsals and on the public stage.

According to the *Continental Gazette*, which is always an excellent authority on such matters, I find that the Parisian theatres are a trifle in advance of us as regards realistic stage effects. It appears that "Le Casque en Fer," which was brought out some months ago at the Château d'Eau, was furnished with genuine flashes of lightning, obtained from a large electrical apparatus set up in the side scenes.

If French theatres are in advance of us in realism, we can scarcely cope with them in point of variety, as the following statistics will prove.

Between the 16th of September, 1879, and the 15th of September, 1880, the Paris Folies Bergères gave three hundred and sixty-four representations, the only night upon which the theatre was closed being Good Friday. During this space of time it offered to the public two hundred and twelve novelties, the detailed list of which is as follows :—Fifteen ballets, eight pantomimes, one marionette theatre, one American rifleman (Dr. Carver), one illusionist prestidigitateur, one man fish, one tamer of crocodiles, one instantaneous painter, ten virtuoso soloists, two jugglers, Egyptian and Japanese, two stuffed ourang-outangs, one living man of the woods, one trio of gnomes humouristic, five troupes of eccentric dancers and singers, eight equilibrists, nine aërial gymnasts, Icarian voltigeurs, and others, three velocipedists, of whom one was an ascensionist, one skater on wheels, one kraal of genuine Zulus, five troupes of learned animals, including one ox and two elephants, two clowns, two athletes, ten marches, twenty-two musical fantasias, nine quadrilles, thirty-one overtures, twenty-three valses, three galops, eleven polkas, seven mazurkas, one orchestra of Taiganes, one company of Spanish mandolinists (L'Estudiantana). If variety is pleasing, the above must have proved a delightful treat.

CHAPTER XV.

FRENCH DRAMATISTS UNSUCCESSFUL WHEN ATTEMPTING TO DELINEATE ENGLISH MANNERS—ENGLISH ACTORS AT THE PORTE ST. MARTIN—TALMA—LE KAIN—MADEMOISELLE MARS —DRAMATIC CENSOR—HECTOR MALET—CRITICISM ON THE ENGLISH DRAMA AND ENGLISH ARTISTS.

Quant à ses défauts, on les excusera sans doute, si l'on considère que l'esprit humain ne peut de tous côtés franchir les bornes qu'opposent à ses efforts le ton du siècle, les mœurs, et les préjugés.

MARMONTEL.

FRENCH dramatic authors have seldom proved successful when attempting to delineate English usages, manners, and customs, notably so in the case of Alexandre Dumas, who brought out a piece at the Variétés entitled "Kean," whom he represented as the intimate friend of the Prince of Wales, afterwards George IV., and his rival in the affections of the ladies of the Court. The drama was in itself interesting, had it not been for the above-mentioned anachronism. In "Richard Darlington" the celebrated election at Liverpool between Denison and Ewart is introduced, though greatly exaggerated, one of the candidates having orange for his colours—those were the days when ribbons were allowed to be given away wholesale, as emblematical of the gold the candidate was about to lavish on the free and independent electors of that borough. There were, however, many exceptions to the above rule, more especially in a piece entitled "Les Anglaise pour rire," an admirable skit on English manners and dress, most cleverly acted by Brunet and Potier.

The French and English stage differ so widely that almost every attempt of an English performer to appear on the Parisian boards has proved unsuccessful. Not so with regard to our Continental neighbours, who for years have come over to London to delight and enlighten the British public. Latterly the speculation has proved highly remunerative, not alone to the *entrepreneur*, but to the *corps dramatique*.

Here I am reminded that towards the end of July, 1822, a company of English actors proceeded to Paris, with a view of appearing at the Porte St. Martin Theatre in the tragedy of "Othello;" but the pittites, whose voices are potential, determined to have their revenge for an insult offered to a French company in the previous generation, and drive the foreign intruders off the stage. In addition to the above-mentioned insult, they were reminded that as late as the year 1763 some French dancers, who appeared in a ballet entitled "Fêtes Chinoises," had been equally ill-treated by a brutal mob, despite the presence of George II., and the exertions of the highest orders to silence the ruffians. When the English actors commenced the performance of "Othello," a dreadful riot ensued, which was only quelled by the appearance of a body of gendarmes, the commander of which gave the order to prime and load, threatening to fire should the tumult continue. If I remember aright, the English company above alluded to were not the best representatives of the British drama.

In 1827 another attempt was made by a superior company, with a much more satisfactory result, as they were most cordially received, not only by the public at large, but by their theatrical *confrères*. Among the leaders of this second company may be mentioned Miss Smithson, Charles Kemble, Abbott, and others whose names have escaped my memory. Upon the occasion of Charles Kemble appearing as Othello, the theatre was honoured by the presence of La Duchesse de Berri. His acting of the jealous Moor produced rapturous applause, except in the scene where he smothers Desdemona, when hisses and groans both loud and deep marked the decided distaste the audience had to witness the murder on the stage.

The French critics in those days objected to assassination on the mimic boards, so that

Horace, in Corneille's tragedy, when he kills his sister, runs after her, and murders her in the side scenes, groans and shrieks from the *coulisses* being allowable, so that the deed be hid from public gaze. This mawkish sentiment no longer exists, for in many modern French dramas deeds of atrocity, murder, suicide, and poisoning are to be met with.

Miss Smithson delighted the audience by her performance of Jane Shore, and was presented with two splendid vases of Sèvres porcelain by the Vicomte de Rochefoucauld, understood to have been given by La Duchesse de Berri.

Sorry I am to have to record an instance, a solitary one, in which Edmund Kean forgot the respect he owed to the nation which was anxious to honour his talent. In 1828 the theatre was crowded in every part to witness his performance of Othello. Seven o'clock struck, and Kean had not made his appearance. Messengers were sent off in every direction in search of the Moor of Venice, and at length he was discovered at the Café Anglais, imbibing draughts of champagne mixed with cognac brandy. His reply to those who sought him was an apostrophe a little too energetic to be repeated here.

"But the Duchesse de Berri has arrived," said one.

"I am not the servant of the Duchess," hiccoughed Kean. "More wine."

At length the manager appealed to him, happily, not in vain. Supported by two waiters he was carried off to the theatre, was dressed, and shortly afterwards made his appearance, but in such a state of inebriety as completely to mar the beauties of Shakespeare.

Since that period other English artists have visited Paris; among them the late Charles Mathews, who delighted the audience by his exquisite performance, both in French and English.

I first met Talma, the unrivalled French tragedian, during the winter of 1814, when I was an *attaché* to the English Ambassador, the late Duke of Wellington. His Grace had a private box at the Théâtre Français, and through the courtesy of the director I was admitted behind the scenes.

François Joseph Talma was unquestionably, in my opinion, one of the greatest actors I ever saw. His voice and action were well adapted for French tragedy; and no one studied what is termed "the business of the part" more than he did. Instead of remaining in the green-room, or standing behind the scenes, ready to be called on, as most actors do, Talma would walk slowly up and down, practising the attitudes he was about to display, and it is reported that, just before he went on in "Hamlet," he would seize hold of some supernumerary by the collar and exclaim:

"Fuis, spectre épouvantable.
Porte au fond des tombeaux ton aspect redoutable."

In Orestes he was as grand as John Kemble was in "Coriolanus." No one devoted himself more to the study of the author than Talma; for days before he appeared in a new part he would lock himself up in his room, denying himself to all visitors. It was to his persevering energy that the reform in costume, commenced by Le Kain, was brought about; previous to this Romans, Greeks, Turks, and Chinese appeared with powdered heads.

In comedy the actresses took their dresses either from *Le Journal des Modes*, or, scorning all reference to the period in which the scene was laid, wore dresses of the time of Louis XV. or Louis XVI. Talma was the first to adopt the Brutus headdress; others shortly followed suit.

I had the good fortune to be present at Talma's benefit in 1825, which took place at the Académie Royale de Musique. It was attended by an immense audience, eager to testify their respect for the great tragedian. Notwithstanding the increase of prices, every place had been pre-engaged for several days, and pit-tickets were sold on the morning of the performance for fifty francs. The play was "Othello," partly taken from the English by Ducis, but unquestionably one of his worst productions. Indeed, nothing but the transcendent powers of Talma could have saved the tragedy. The character of Iago, one of Shakespeare's finest conceptions, is omitted, and is replaced by a mean, shuffling Cesare, in every respect inferior to the deep, designing villain of the English stage. The costumes were splendid, but the play, at least to my ears, was dull and vapid, with the exception of those scenes in which the Moor of Venice appeared.

I had not seen this great artist since the year 1816, but there was no diminution of his wonderful powers. The receipts of the evening above referred to amounted to upwards of thirty thousand francs.

This was the last time I saw Talma, for he died on the 19th of October in the following year, in the sixty-first year of his age.

His funeral, which took place at Père-la-Chaise, was attended by a large concourse of people, and by all the members of the Théâtre Français.

Le Kain, above referred to, was called "Le

restaurateur des costumes," and no less deserved the title of "Bienfaiteur de la Comédie et des Comédians." He succeeded in putting an end to the custom, so detrimental to the actor, so destructive to scenic effect, of allowing a portion of the audience to appear on the stage. A row of seats, similar to the stalls now introduced in English and French theatres, was taken from the pit to accommodate those who had patronized the scenic benches.

Voltaire's play of "L'Orphélin de la Chine," produced at the Théâtre Français in 1755, was the first play in which all the actors appeared in the proper costume of the characters they represented. Though Le Kain and Mademoiselle Clairon had begun and continued this reform, there were actors and actresses who, because of the expense of a new and greatly varied wardrobe, could only follow their example by slow degrees. Moreover, some actresses could not resist the temptation of displaying whatever diamonds and other jewels they possessed, no matter what character they were playing. Thus a *soubrette* would appear bedizened as a duchess, and a *paysan* discoursed of her humble home and honest poverty amidst a blaze of diamonds.

Some actors, too, liked to fancy themselves for a brief space *des vrais talons rouges* (Adam was once represented wearing that distinguished *chaussure* of the *haute noblesse*), with silk stockings, diamond knee buckles, lace cravat, ruffles, and sword.

"L'Orphélin" was successful, despite Fréron's malignant criticism, uniformity and propriety of costume being no doubt greatly in its favour.

Having referred to the great tragedian Talma, I now approach an equally talented artist of bygone days, Mademoiselle Mars. This lady, who combined all the vivacity of a Jordan with the grace and elegance of a Farren, was equally great in high as in low comedy. Her Charlotte in "Tartuffe," and Betty in "La Jeunesse de Henri Cinq," were unapproachable. "La Jeunesse de Henri Cinq" is founded on the

English drama of "Charles the Second." To account for the inconsistency of introducing the wicked Earl of Rochester as the companion of "Sweet King Hal," I may remark that when the drama was first about to be brought out at Paris, during the reign of Napoleon I., the licencer objected to Charles as being a restored monarch, so that the author had no alternative left him but to re-write the whole, or change his hero. The latter course he adopted, trusting that a Parisian audience would not detect the anachronism.

Here I may remark that there exists in Paris, and has existed for years, a dramatic censor, who exercises the same powers that the Lord Chamberlain does in England. It appears that in 1702 Louis XIV., through the Marquis de Gervres, reprimanded the actors for taking great liberties in a comedy entitled "Bal D'Auteuil;" from that moment a licenser was appointed to read every play before it could be represented. Previous to this, so long ago as 1442, the Parliament put a check to the licentiousness of some of the dramas; but I will content myself with modern instances.

In 1789 the Mayor of Paris was invested with authority to act in conjunction with four gentlemen attached to the Court as censors over the drama in Paris. In the provinces the duties fell upon the municipal authorities, whose experience in theatricals was extremely limited, but who exercised in an alarming manner their brief authority. At Toulouse, the capitoul, or sheriff, was highly incensed when, in the " Metromanie " of Piron, the following line was delivered, which he took for a personal affront, he not being at all inflicted with giddiness in the head:—" Monsieur le Capitoul, vous avez des vertiges."

Another French sheriff ordered the author of " L'Avare," whose name he understood to be Molière, to be arrested, because he considered the scene in which Harpagon is robbed by his own son was meant to apply to his own family. When he learnt that it was impossible to put the decree into execution, Molière having been defunct many years previously, the Capitoul replied,

"Why do they give us comedies written by unknown authors?"

Again an author gave the name of Dubois to a thief in one of his pieces; unfortunately for him the Prefect of Police was named Dubois. The censor immediately wrote to the official to say that he had erased the name of Dubois, out of respect for him, not wishing to allow the name of the scourge of thieves to be prostituted by a thief.

To return to Mademoiselle Mars, with whom I was personally acquainted, and who was as *spirituelle* in private life as she was clever upon the stage.

In the year 1815, after the return of the Bourbons, the Gardes du Corps at Paris raised a great cabal against this lady, who was known to be a staunch Napoleonist, and they made a party to drive her off the stage. Being told of this, she naïvely replied,

"What can these gentlemen of the Gardes du Corps hold in common with *Mars?*"

When she appeared at night, in a dress ornamented with bees and violets, the Napoleon symbols, she was met with groans and hisses. Not condescending to address the audience, and explain the motives attributed to her, she remained silent. At length the tumult was so great, and the demand made upon her to cry "Vive la Roi!" so appalling, that to prevent any further riot she said, with simplicity,

"I have cried 'Vive le Roi!' during the disturbance."

After this the performance was allowed to proceed without any further disturbance.

Hector Malot, in his amusing work, "La Vie Moderne en Angleterre," thus describes the British stage:—

"England, which abounds in literature of the highest class, as regards romance, criticisms, history, and science, has no dramatic literature, and it is an incontestable fact that the French theatre has immolated the English theatre. For many years translations of French pieces were unknown in England, and for the most part those produced were original. Many of these original dramas did not produce any great influence on the British public, and were certainly not *chefd'œuvres* at the same period. France, though rich in the works of Molière, Beaumarchais, and Corneille, preferred the modern dramas of Victor Hugo and Alexandre Dumas, the comedies of Scribe, the vaudevilles of Bayard, and even the farces of Duvert and Lausanne.

"The English managers, aware of the success of modern French dramatists, preferred the translations of the above to original works. This system was unquestionably advantageous, as they risked little or nothing. Selecting those pieces which had been stamped with popularity by a Parisian audience, they anticipated the same result on the English boards, and, moreover, saved themselves the expense of paying large sums for original plays. For the last fifty years every successful piece played in Paris has been played in London, many of which have been condemned, altered, and arranged to suit the taste of the English."

The writer then proceeds to say that the English theatre is in a very singular position, neither dead nor alive, uncertain—"*se débattant dans le vide.*"

After a due appreciation of "Colleen Bawn," "The Octoroon," and "Our American Cousin," the latter a severe satire on the aristocracy, which nightly invokes the laughter and applause of the middle classes, who, during the day, pay abject homage to those of rank, Monsieur Malot tells us that, although the splendid creations of Shakespeare are played everywhere, they, like those of Racine and Corneille in France, fail to draw audiences. He then tells us that the present system of translating French pieces has not produced many modern remarkable actors. He makes exception in favour of Mr. Phelps, who, he considers, is without a rival, Sothern, Boucicault, the late Robson, Poole, Wigan, Widdicombe, and Buckstone.

Hector Malot thus refers to Charles Mathews, but I rather think he has mixed up the inimitable Mathews the elder with his son.

He says:

"There is one name that ought not to be omitted, it is that of Charles Mathews. Unfortunately, Mathews, wearied with acting comic characters, has retired from the stage to give a monologue, entitled 'Mathews at Home,' which, as report says, is a representation extremely original; for, with a versatility of talent peculiar to himself, he represents and imitates almost every actor, English, French and Italian."

To the above a note is added by the author, which evidently applies to the worthy scion of the above most worthy sire. It runs as follows:

"To those who consider me too severe upon the British stage, its actors, authors, and the public, I must lay before my readers a conversation I had with Mr. Mathews. Being astonished with his pronunciation of the French language, which is thoroughly pure, I asked him why he never acted in Paris.

"'It is the dream of my youth, the fondest

wish of my heart,' he replied; 'and I would give years of my life to do so.'

"I cannot understand why he should not have realized this dream. Mr. Mathews has sufficient talent to take rank on our stage amongst our best actors of comedy."

We rather think this dream was realized, and that the late Charles Mathews fully merited Hector Malot's eulogium.

Of Charles Kean he says he possesses the name of his father alone. This I think unjust and illiberal; for in many characters Charles Kean was excellent. Of Fechter's Hamlet, Hector Malot remarks that he adds to the English diction the horrible melodramatic rant of the Porte St. Martin Theatre. This is equally unjust; in tenderness few excelled Fechter.

Clever actresses, he declares, are as scarce as clever actors, adding that he is not sufficiently acquainted with the merits or demerits of all to give a decided opinion; but, as far as his experience goes, he considers

Mrs. Charles Kean to possess the highest dramatic talent, and that Madame Boucicault cannot be better characterised than by describing her as *une bouffe femme,* who possesses that most precious of all qualities—charms.

Hector concludes his chapter on the English stage with the following remarks:

"In the present day, with the exception of those concerned in the ballet, the life of actors is in every respect irreproachable; it is one of the most quiet and honourable character. To marry is their only ambition; and to bring up their children in a respectable manner their only occupation. As for talent, alas! it is difficult to be found."

Here I must remark, first, that I consider Monsieur Hector Malot is too severe on those employed in the ballet, for when we consider their youth and the temptations they are exposed to, it speaks highly for them that few have swerved from the path of *virtue;* next, I would observe that the British stage is not deficient in first-rate actors, artists that could vie with those of other nations as regards their talent. It would be invidious to select any for especial commendation, but I leave it to the reader to fill up in his own mind the list of those who have enraptured him by their talents.

CHAPTER XVI.

"THE RAMBLER'S" OPINION OF MISS SMITHSON—BERLIOZ—HIS DEVOTION TO THE BEAUTIFUL ARTIST—AN ILL-FATED MARRIAGE—"HANDS, NOT HEARTS."

> She sits, like beauty's child, whom nature got
> For man to see, and seeing wonder at.
> SHAKESPEARE.

> The hearts, of old, gave hands;
> But our new Heraldry is hands, not hearts.
> SHAKESPEARE.

UNDER the title of "The Rambler" the following interesting article appeared in *The Parisian* :—

"While book-hunting along the quays (of Paris) the other day, I discovered in a dusty portfolio an old lithograph by Francis, dated

1827, and representing Miss Smithson and Mr. Charles Kemble in 'Romeo and Juliet.' The history of the triumphs of Miss Smithson at Paris in the early part of this century was related at length in a series of articles published in *The Parisian* last year. Miss Smithson's name used to be in everybody's mouth, and the Irish beauty *fêted* and applauded almost as much as Sarah Bernhardt was before she abandoned Paris in order to become a wandering 'star.' In England Miss Smithson had met with little success; her Irish brogue was against her. But here in Paris people did not notice the brogue, and were struck only by her beauty and grace. In the lithograph I found Miss Smithson etherealised and spiritualised in a manner which alone, even if the lithograph were not signed and dated, would mark it as the composition of an idealist of the high romantic school. It must have been done at the time of Miss Smithson's first appearance in Paris, in the summer of 1827.

"The performance of the plays of Shakespeare came as a revelation to the young men of those days, and the battle of the Romanticists against the Classicists was fought over again in the press at each new piece that the English actors played.

"Victor Hugo and Lamartine were amongst the assiduous frequenters of the Théâtre Anglais, and Hector Berlioz was so bewitched with Shakespeare that he determined to do for music what Victor Hugo had done for poetry. Berlioz was not less bewitched with Miss Smithson than he was with Shakespeare. He raved about her beauty as ardently as he swore by Shakespeare. At that time Berlioz was a young man of brilliant talent, seeking his path, and finding himself, like all the Romanticists, out of harmony with the old order of things; and, not quite knowing what the new order was to be, Shakespeare dawned upon him like a revelation. The early years of his life at Paris had been full of privations; he had lived on bread and dried fruits, until at last he obtained a situation as *choriste*, at fifty francs a month, at the Théâtre des Nouveautés.

"This was for him a period of great enthusiasms, of ardent passions, of infinite joys. It was in this moment of musical hallucination that he became acquainted with Weber's genius in 'Der Freischütz,' with that of Glück in 'Iphigénie en Tauride,' with that of Spontini in 'La Vestale'; it was then, when he had barely reached the age of twenty-four, that the poetical Miss Smithson appeared to him in the white dress of Ophelia; it was then that he recognized true grandeur, true beauty, and dramatic truth.

" 'Shakespeare,' he writes, 'coming upon me thus unexpectedly, struck me like a thunderbolt. I saw, I comprehended, I felt that I was living, and that I must rise up and walk.'

" He did rise up and walk, and, with the audacity of youthful genius, he tried to accomplish the impossible. He wished to be noble and majestic like Spontini, fantastic like Weber, gentle and mild like Virgil or Phorintus, trivial and sublime like Shakespeare, and grand like Beethoven. His passion for Miss Smithson, to whom he was unknown, caused him to pass through a terrible crisis, and finally it became a spur that urged him to work. He would make himself known by his talent to her who had charmed him by her beauty. With this end he organized a concert. It was 'Love's Labour Lost.' Miss Smithson, not knowing even the name of her obscure slave, did not appear at the *fête* that had been prepared in her honour. Cruel deception! But, as if by way of prosaic recompense, the newspapers mentioned the concert; it was the first time that he had appealed to the judgment of the critics, and it was favourable to him. He had, therefore, only to continue working. He went to Rome to the French Academy, where he met Mendelssohn, that perfect gentleman, who was a little shocked at the Bohemianism and violent principles of the young French Romanticist.

"In his correspondence, Mendelssohn speaks of Berlioz as 'a veritable caricature, without a shadow of talent, feeling his way in the darkness, and believing himself the creator of the world; besides that, he writes the most detestable things, and talks and dreams only of Beethoven, Schiller, and Goethe. He is also a man of incommensurable vanity, and treats with superb disdain Mozart and Haydn, so that all his enthusiasm seems to be very suspicious.'

"Nevertheless, the relations of Berlioz and Mendelssohn at Rome were almost intimate, and if it had not been for the wide difference of national character—a difference which, especially in the case of French artists and men of letters, always makes it difficult for foreigners to get on with them—Berlioz and Mendelssohn would certainly have thoroughly appreciated each other. Both of them professed the same respect for the great geniuses of music, and, above all, both of them were ardent admirers of Shakespeare, whose ideas they were both destined to translate into music with equal happiness, the one in his 'Songe d'une Nuit d'Eté,' and the other in his 'Romeo et Juliette.'

"While at Rome at the Villa Medici, with his head full of Shakespeare, Goethe, and Walter Scott, Berlioz wrote 'Le Retour à la Vie,' 'La

Ballade du Pêcheur,' 'Rob Roy,' and especially the ghost scene in 'Hamlet,' and the overture of his 'Roy Lear.' In 1832 he returned to Paris, and his concerts, at which he had executed all the strange symphonies that rang in his romantic head, procured him that ineffable joy which he had sought in vain three years before. The sudden glory that surrounded a new name attracted the attention of Henrietta Smithson, and, touched by the ardour of the young composer's patient passion, she gave him her hand, and the marriage was celebrated soon afterwards, in spite of the opposition of the family of Berlioz, who foresaw the unhappiness of the union, contracted in a moment of artistic fever.

"The marriage did turn out unhappily: At first fortune refused to smile upon the couple. It was not, indeed, until after the performance of the symphony of 'Harold en Italie,' composed for Paganini, that the talent of Berlioz was recognized even by a few serious connoisseurs. Henceforward, however, he began to progress both in fame and fortune. According to Monsieur Legouvé, who has recently spoken of Berlioz in his 'Souvenirs,' Madame Berlioz was very cold in her love at first, while Berlioz himself was raging with torrid passion. Then, as Madame Berlioz began to know her husband better, her love became stronger. Unfortunately, Hector's passion began to cool down gradually, until finally the rôles were inverted, and Hector was very cool when Madame Berlioz had become very ardent. Meanwhile, Berlioz was becoming famous, and his connection with theatrical people caused his wife to become furiously jealous. Finally, life in common became no longer possible. They separated by mutual consent, and Berlioz continued his agitated career alone.

"His biographers have represented Berlioz as an *incompris* whose efforts were not recognised at all during his lifetime. His life was, it is true, to some extent embittered by the disdain and mockery of his contemporaries, but his bitterness was due largely to his own strange and wayward nature. His life was a life of struggle. As M. F. Thomas said, in his discourse over Berlioz's grave, 'God had given him that sacred fire which makes enthusiasm, and he himself had contributed that obstinate will and that active patience which are the signs and characteristics of genius.'

"Berlioz's glory is the glory of militant genius —a glory perhaps destined to be more lasting than that, for instance, of Victor Hugo, who has been inhaling the incense of undisputed fame since he first began to write.

"After the separation, Berlioz and his wife remained good friends, and he frequently wrote to see her as a friend in her retirement at Montmartre. The offspring of this union was a son, to whom Berlioz was deeply attached, and whose death preceded that of his father by only a few months. The lady, who, as Miss Smithson, had been for years the rival in the favour of the public of the famous Mademoiselle Mars, ended her days in the saddest of all widowhoods, the isolation of the *femme séparée*.

"Such is the outline of the tragic tale that

hangs by the old lithograph that I found on the quay."

I have given this long extract because I feel that it will deeply interest all "old stagers" who, like myself, witnessed Miss Smithson's triumphs in Paris and England.

I only regret that I am not acquainted with the name of the writer of the above admirable and touching sketch of the ill-fated son and daughter of genius, or I would tender him my personal thanks and congratulations.

My acquaintance with Miss Smithson began when Mr. Ball Hughes (commonly called "The Golden Ball") was anxious to display his histrionic powers at an amateur performance which was to take place at the Tottenham Court Theatre, now the Prince of Wales's. The play he chose was "Richard the Third," selecting the part of the "crooked-back tyrant" for himself, the remaining male characters being by amateurs, of whom I was one, the female ones by professional ladies. Being on terms of friendship with Mr. and Mrs. Orger, I spoke to them upon the subject, when Mrs. Orger suggested Miss Smithson for Lady Anne, and kindly consenting to take the other part herself.

The afterpiece was to be "The Mayor of Garratt," in which I was to appear as Major Sturgeon, and a cousin of mine, who, I am happy to say, still is "in the land of the living," was to be Jerry Sneak.

"But who will undertake the two female characters?" I asked.

"Let me arrange that with Miss Smithson. I have no doubt that she will, like myself, be too happy to forward any views of yours."

This was accordingly arranged. Abbott, of Covent Garden Theatre, was retained by Ball Hughes to teach him the part; Angelo was to give him lessons in fencing, that the encounter with Richmond on the battle-field might produce an effect; and I secured the services of the above ladies.

Nothing could exceed their attention at rehearsals, and all was going on in a flourishing manner when some of the *corps dramatique* became suddenly ill, or rather *indisposed* to appear before the public. At the dress-rehearsal we had admitted some friends of Mrs. Orger and Miss Smithson, and a few of our own; this so terrified three of the amateurs that they felt it impossible to face a larger audience, so, at the last moment, the programme was given up.

CHAPTER XVII.

TALMA IN "BRITANNICUS"—MADEMOISELLE GEORGES AS THE EMPRESS AGRIPPINA—FRENCH PATRIOTISM—MARSHAL NEY—PIECES DE CIRCONSTANCE—FULSOME COMPLIMENTS.

> Exact Racine and Corneille's noble fire
> Showed us that France had something to admire.
> . . . .
> 'Tis he who gives my breast a thousand pains,
> Can make me feel each passion that he feigns;
> Enrage, compose with more than magic art,
> With pity and with terror tear my heart,
> And snatch me o'er the earth, or through the air,
> To Thebes, to Athens, when he will, and where.
> POPE.

AMONG other tragedies which I saw performed at the Théâtre Français was "Britannicus," a piece described by Racine as the one upon which he had devoted most labour and study. Thus recommended by its author, and sustained by Talma as Nero, Mademoiselle Georges, and the whole strength of the company, my most anxious expectations were awakened; nor was I disappointed, for nothing could exceed the histrionic ability of Talma as Nero, and of Mademoiselle Georges as the Roman Empress Agrippina. Nothing could exceed the dignity and tragic powers of Talma, or the clearness of diction, elegance of enunciation, graceful calmness of action, dignity of gesture, majesty, beauty, and symmetry of Mademoiselle Georges.

Mademoiselle Duchesnois was exquisitely pathetic. Of her it may be said, "L'art n'est pas fait pour elle, elle n'en a pas besoin." Mistress of all the softer passions, I have known even those who did not understand a word she uttered moved to tears at her performance.

I have referred in a former chapter upon English theatricals to patriotism indulged in upon the stage; here I must record an instance of loyal demonstration at the Odéon at Paris. It occurred shortly after the death of the brave, ill-fated Marshal Ney. The Odéon Theatre, generally the dullest of all the Parisian theatres, was to be enlivened by the presence of the Duke and Duchess de Berri, to witness " Le Chevalier de Canolle." This piece is founded on a very slight historical fact, in the history of the wars of the Fronde, but in the gallant character of the Chevalier, himself the victim of faction, condemned under the law of reprisal to be publicly executed, the public identified the misfortunes of Marshal Ney.

What gave colour to this supposition was the coincidence of the situation, and the words of the Chevalier and the Marshal a few minutes before their execution. When the fatal hour arrived which was to remove Ney from the prison to the place of execution, the officer on guard found him asleep, and, on awaking him, complimented him on a state of mind which at such a moment enabled him to indulge in a repose so calm and profound. The Marshal replied, with a faint and placid smile, " Je m'essayais," in allusion to that long sleep which awaited him.

In the last act of "Le Chevalier Canolle" he is found asleep by his mistress and his friends, who come to bid him a last farewell a few minutes before his execution. To the observation of his young mistress, "Vous dormiez," he replies, with a smile on his countenance, "Je m'essayais."

The effect was electric; it spread through all parts of the house, despite the vociferous cries of the royalists to quell it by calling for the national air, "Vive Henri Quatre."

The loyal effusions, or rather tasteless, injudicious, and fulsome stuff purchased from hireling poetasters and impecunious scribblers, which disgraced the theatres after the restoration of Louis the Eighteenth, and on the occasion of the Duc de Berri's marriage, were perfectly revolting. These *pièces de circonstance* took possession of the boards which had been immortalised by the *chefd'œuvres* of Corneille, Racine, Voltaire, and Molière, and were founded not only on historical facts connected with the history of the Bourbons, but on the *bonmots, mots de cœur,* and *mots de sentiment* supposed to have been uttered by the restored monarch (irreverently called Louis *Des Huitres,* from his love of the Louis Le Gros, and the *Préfet D'Angleterre*) and his illustrious family. These *pièces de circonstance* were as numerous as the leaves that strewed the Valley of Vallambrosa, in addition to which all the "sayings and doings" of Henri Quatre were dramatised.

Among the *pièces de circonstance* were the following: "Charles du France," "Le Chemin de Fontainebleau," "Une Journée à Versailles," "La Pensée d'un Bon Roi," "Une Soirée aux Tuileries," "L'Impromptu de Provence," "Le Bonheur d'un Bon Roi," "Les Filles à Marier," "Le Roi et la Ligne," &c., &c.

A loyal piece at the Vaudeville, in which the characters were composed of flowers, including the modest snowdrop, the pale primrose, the gaudy tulip, the blooming carnation, the unpretending violet, the beauteous lily, the pretty pansy, the garden's gem, heartsease, was not appreciated by the audience, despite its fulsome compliments to the king, which were laid on with a trowel. Among other speeches, Flora, after crowning the fleur-de-lys queen of the garden, exclaims,

"Je cherchai la vertu, et je trouvais Louis!"

This sentiment was applauded to the echo, but when the queen of the flowers inquired, "Who is that sulky flower that stands in a *morne silence* pouting in the corner?" a sister flower replies that it is the guilty, proscribed, usurping violet, who alone of all the flowers refuses obedience to the fleur-de-lys (the emblem of the Bourbons). At this remark the violet is instantly called into Court, severely reprobated and condemned, but as royal clemency is the order of the day (it was not so when the "bravest of the brave" was shot in the gardens of the Luxembourg), the culprit violet receives the benefit of the amnesty, and joins in a chorus extolling the virtues of Flora and Louis XVIII.

Although the theatre was tolerably well packed with claqueurs pledged to support loyalty upon that occasion, there was a strong feeling on the part of the Napoleonists, and, let us hope, some currency of generous feeling among the royalists that it was cowardly thus publicly to trample on a fallen foe, who so recently had been the idol of the nation. The result was that, after a stormy conflict, the management deemed it expedient to withdraw the piece, and the flowers were nipped in their buds.

CHAPTER XVIII.

CELEBRITIES I HAVE KNOWN—MESDEMOISELLES BOURGOIN, DUCHESNOIS, AND DÉJAZET—LEONTINE VOLNY—LEONTINE FAY, HER NOM DU THÉATRE— ROMANCE OF REAL LIFE.

Voyagez beaucoup, et vous ne trouverez pas de peuple aussi doux, aussi affable, aussi franc, aussi poli, aussi spirituel, que le Français ; il est quelque fois trop, mais ce défaut est-il donc si grand ? Il s'affecte avec vivacité et promptitude, et quelquefois pour des choses très frivoles, tandis que des objets importants, on le touchent peu, on n'excitent qui sa plaisanterie.

RAYNAL.

AMONG the French *artistes* with whom I became acquainted were Mademoiselle Bourgoin and Mademoiselle Duchesnois. Mademoiselle Bourgoin was carried off by a most painful disease during the summer of 1833, and

Mademoiselle Duchesnois died at Paris in 1835, and was attended to the grave by a concourse of literary characters and friends, anxious to pay the last tribute of respect to one of the greatest tragic actresses of the day. Poor Mademoiselle Bourgoin was not only a good actress, but distinguished by her wit and repartees in society, which occasionally outstepped the limits of delicacy.

Upon one occasion, when dining with Baron D——, shortly after he had received a decoration from the King of Prussia, which he was, of course, proud of displaying, as the Jews are seldom favoured with those distinctions, Mademoiselle Bourgoin, the acknowledged object of the Baron's affections, had some trifling difference with her host. This produced a warm discussion between her lover and the lady, who at length became so exasperated that she lost her temper, and said to him, with great bitterness, before the whole of the guests, among them Talma and Lafitte, the banker,

"Maudit Juif, tu portes la croix, et tu renies ton sauveur."

To this there could be no reply.

Mademoiselle Duchesnois made her *début* in the month of July, 1802, with the greatest success, and in the following November, notwithstanding the jealousy and opposition of her rivals at the Théâtre Français, was crowned upon the stage.

It was with the greatest difficulty that this accomplished *artiste* gained permission to make a first appearance at the above theatre. Night after night, modestly attired, she sought an engagement at the hands of the management; and her entreaties were received with disdain and raillery. At her first representation, called before the curtain by the audience, no one was willing to offer her his hand. Monsieur Florence had at last sufficient moral courage to lead Mademoiselle Duchesnois forward, much to the disgust of the other performers.

Some days after Mademoiselle Duchesnois had been crowned on the stage, Mademoiselle

Georges, an *élève* of Mademoiselle Rancourt, and a *protégée* of Madame Louis Bonaparte (afterwards Queen Hortense), made her *début* as Clytemnestre. Gifted with great beauty and intelligence of no mean order, she was deficient in soul and in warmth of feeling. Magnificent as a queen, she lacked the tenderness that should have characterised her delineation of Clytemnestre. Notwithstanding these drawbacks, her friends exerted themselves to the utmost to bring her forward in the characters in which Mademoiselle Duchesnois had established herself, notably in that of Phèdre.

This attempt to crush one who had made so favourable an impression on the public led to a tumult, which was carried on with vehement rancour on both sides. Hisses and cheers assailed the two rival queens from their respective partisans, and this feeling was carried on to the greatest extent behind the scenes as on the boards.

Mademoiselle Rancourt, who naturally supported her *élève*, met with that sibilation so "unpleasant to an actress's ear" when performing in "Iphigénie en Aulide," and attributed it to Mademoiselle Duchesnois. " Elle voulut s'en venger à force ouverte," writes M. de Manne in "La Nouvelle Biographie Générale," when it became necessary to arrest the blow, and protect the slender Eryphile against the more formidable and colossal Clytemnestre.

Had it not been for the intervention of the Empress Josephine, it is probable that Mademoiselle Duchesnois would have succumbed to Mademoiselle Georges and the clique that supported her. Happily, however, Mademoiselle Georges, by her unexpected flight to Vienna, and subsequently to Russia, left the field open for her rival.

Mademoiselle Déjazet, who created a great sensation at the French plays got up under the superintendence of that popular librarian, the late Mr. Mitchell, of Bond Street, at the St. James's Theatre, was, to my mind, one of the cleverest *artistes* in a particular line of business that I ever saw. I once saw her at the Théâtre du Palais Royal, in a light, trifling piece by Messrs. Villeneuve and Livry, entitled " Voltaire en Vacances," in which she represented the part of the young poet. It referred to the period when Voltaire was in love with Ninon. His talent, though in its infancy, was beginning to burst forth, and one of his first efforts appears in a petition to the King on behalf of a deserving old soldier, who rewarded it by granting a pension :

> "Sire, vous possédez d'assez bons revenus,
> Car vous avez, dit-on, cent millions de rente,
> Exempts d'impôts et de patente,
> Ce que fait à peu près par jour cent mille écus,
> Ou bien quatre mille par heure.
> Moi, qui vous ai servi vingt ans,
> Ne pourrois-je obtenir, Sire, avant que je meure,
> Un quart d'heure de votre temps!"

Perhaps one of Déjazet's greatest triumphs was in "Vert Vert," founded on one of La Fontaine's fables, and "La Marquise de Prétintaille," taken from Beranger.

Among other delightful French actresses may be mentioned Leontine Volny, better known in the dramatic world as Leontine Fay. This pleasing and excellent artist was the heroine of a romantic story in real life. Fascinating in her manners, and pleasing in her person, though not strikingly handsome, she inspired a violent attachment in a young man, son of Count Montalivet, the minister, who, finding all his hopes of happiness centred in a union with Leontine, formally proposed to marry her. Though flattered by his addresses, she still refused to listen to his offer, unless sanctioned by the approbation of his family, which no entreaties on his part could ever procure from his parents, who were violently opposed to the marriage.

To extinguish all hope in her young admirer, and to avoid every suspicion of encouraging an attachment in opposition to the wishes and injunctions of his friends, she wrote to Monsieur Volny, who on a former occasion had made her an unsuccessful offer of his hand, that, if he still entertained the same predilection for her, she now was willing to accept his proposal.

He received her overtures with undiminished

attachment, and she shortly afterwards became his wife. But the young Montalivet's passion was not to be subdued by these insurmountable obstacles; he suddenly went abroad, and shortly afterwards put a period to his own existence.

CHAPTER XIX.

FRENCH MANAGERS ADOPT THE SYSTEM OF ENGLISH STROLLING MANAGERS OF CHANGING THE TITLE OF PLAYS—TECHNOLOGIE THÉATRALE, OR GREEN-ROOM PHRASEOLOGY.

Dans la suite du Roman comique, nous lisons ceci à propos de la reception de Ragotin dans la troupe nomade. "On lui donna le mot auquel tous les comédiens se reconnaissent." Cette phrase indique l'existence d'une espece de francmaçonnerie entre les acteurs. De la à l'argot, il n'y a qu'un pas.

S'il n'y a plus aujourd'hui de mot d'ordre auquel tous les comédiens se reconnaissent, de langue cabalistique et francmaçonnique qui leur serve de point de ralliement il y a du moins encore, et il y aura toujours, l'argot du métier, souvent assez obseur, que pour les profanes ne puissent comprendre sans explication.

V. FOURNEL.

I HAVE in a former chapter remarked that in England many a manager of a strolling company has announced plays under very different titles from those which they originally bore. Thus I myself have seen "The Honeymoon" acted as "The Proud Lady of Seville, or Pride Must Have a Fall," and I have no doubt that other plays have received similar appellations. This system has, however, not been confined exclusively to our native isle, for our Continental neighbours adopted it in bygone days, and probably continue it to the present time.

The celebrated Volange, who, with his troupe, visited almost every town in France, was famed for his talent in renaming pieces. Instead of announcing "Zaïre," he called it "The Amorous and Jealous Grand Turk;" "Beverley," probably founded on our "Gamester," he entitled "The Fatal Effect of the Passion of Gambling." At Brives-la-Gaillard he announced "The Interrupted Voyage" as "The Young Man of Brives-la-Gaillard;" at Villeneuve-sur-Yonne he converted "The Collateral" into "The Seller of Wood of Villeneuve-sur-Yonne." "The Diligence" was named after the towns he visited—" The Diligence of Joigny," of "Rheims," of "Fontainebleau," etc., etc. At Dijon he called a celebrated drama of Mercier's "The Vinegar Merchant of Dijon;" at Villers-Cotterets "The Misanthrope" appeared in the bills as "The Misanthrope of Villers-Cotterets." "Se non è vero, è ben trovato."

Volange possessed a wonderful instinct for ascertaining in what town the author of any popular piece was born, or had been connected with. When he failed in this he would boldly aver that the drama he was about to play was the production of a citizen of the town in which he and his *corps dramatique* found themselves. After announcing, with truth, "The Plaideurs, by Racine, native of Teste-Milon," he announced the same play by M. Racine, native of Château Thierry.

In a small rural village he had the effrontery to announce Molière's "Le Médicin malgré Lui" as a comedy from the pen of a young author belonging to the Commune; nay, so far did he carry his charlatanism that in another provincial town he announced "Le Tartuffe" as a comedy in five acts, by M. Scribe.

The French drama has become so great an institution in London that it may not only be interesting, but may be profitable to those who patronize Mr. Hollingshead's splendid performances at the Gaiety Theatre, if I lay before them the "argot," or theatrical slang of the French coulisses.

For the following *Technologie Théâtrale* I am indebted to a most able and interesting work by V. Fournel, entitled "Curiosités Théâtrales, Anciennes et Modernes, Françaises et Etrangères." I omit many phrases because they are of local Parisian interest, referring to the names of performers who have identified themselves with a line of characters they have made their own, such for instance as "Les Michot" and "Les Dugazon," named after a celebrated actor and actress. To commence alphabetically.

"*Attraper le lustre*" is to open the mouth, and utter a sound which gives the throat pain.

"*Battre des ailes*" applies to an actor who makes frequent gestures with his arms, and strikes his body violently, to give strength to his passion. M. Marty is said to have carried this to so great an extent that he was compelled to retire from the stage before two years had elapsed. What human chest could receive with impunity ninety-two blows given during one burst of anger.

"*Bruler les planches,*" to act with unwonted fire and vivacity.

"*Cabotin,*" a strolling actor; a term derived from the nautical verb *caboter*, to sail along the coast, and trade from port to port, or from one *Cabotina*, a quack doctor, vendor of drugs, and an actor of farces.

"*Chauffer la scène,*" to keep the audience alive by animated acting.

"*Comparses.*" Figurants, who, when required, are transformed into heroes, who don the helmet, the cuirass, appear in coats of mail, armed with muskets, cartridge-boxes, bows, and clubs, each fancying himself Alexander the Great at twenty pence a day. The *Chef de Comparses* directed the manœuvres, enforced discipline among the janissaries, received half a franc a day, and had the power of levying and appropriating any fines on acts of insubordination.

"*Claque*" is a term that requires little explanation; the *Claqueurs* in France were of all classes.

"*Les Claqueurs Romains;*" so called from their being united after the manner of the Roman legions.

"*Les Chevaliers de lustre,*" from the place they occupied in the theatre, near the chandelier; they had a well organized staff of a chief and lieutenants; the body consisted of intimate friends and habitual *claqueurs*, all of whom entered the theatre gratuitously.

There were also the "*Lavables,*" from laver to wash, in theatrical slang to sell, who paid a low price for their admission, and the "*Solitaires,*" amateurs, who, to save the crush, and secure good places followed the *claqueurs* in, paid for their seats, and were not permitted to hiss.

"*Côtelettes;*" applause.

"*Doublures,*" synonymous with our "Doubles," actors who double their characters.

"*Les Ganaches, ou Pères Dindons;*" imbecile and garrulous old men.

"*Les jeunes premiers;*" good-looking youthful actors, destined to love and be loved whenever they appear on the boards.

"*Les Queues rouges;*" low buffoons.

"*En avoir;*" a term adopted by actresses to signify a rich lover.

"*Enfoncer,*" to fail in success; applicable alike to actors and dramatic pieces.

"*Escamoter le mot,*" to slur over a word that might be deemed objectionable by a fastidious audience.

"*Etoile;*" similar to our "star."

"*Faire,*" to make a piece. "It is I who made M. Scribe's pieces," exclaimed Soutou, the chief of *claqueurs*.

"*Faire de la toile,*" to get bewildered, and not to know what to say.

"*La toile fine*" is applied to a clever actor, who, for a moment forgetting his part, fills up the time, until the prompter, "though lost to sight, to memory dear," gives him the word.

The term "*Faire du canevas*" is applicable to him who entirely fails in memory, and has not intelligence enough to fill up the vacancy.

"*Feu, feux;*" high salaries.

"*Faire fourre*" is said of a piece looked upon as likely to attract, but which is doomed to be condemned.

"*La Grande Casaque*" includes characters similar to My Lord Duke and Sir Harry, in "High Life below Stairs," who exclaim:

"What wretches are ordinary servants that go on in the same vulgar track every day, eating, working, and sleeping; but we who have the honour to serve the nobility are of another species: we are above the common forms, have servants to wait on us, and are as lazy and luxurious as our masters."

"*Lancer le trait;*" a term applied to those comedians who make brilliant points and hits.

"*Manger les côtelettes;*" to obtain a triumph, and be rewarded by applause.

"*Montrer la couture de ses bas;*" to break an engagement.

"*Une tanne;*" an insignificant character.

"*Perdre son bâton;*" to be in a bad temper.

"*Faire son public;*" this is said of an actress who, with an expressive eye, appears to claim indulgence with head erect, the hands crossed, and trembling voice, with graceful curtseys, sings the last verse of an opera or operetta; similar, for instance, to the Princess of Navarre's couplet in "John of Paris:"

> "Ah me, those eyes of heavenly blue
> Proclaim a heart as fond as true.
> I'd barter all the world to be
> So dearly loved, if loved by thee."

"*Recevoir son morceau de sucre;*" applied to artists who, on their appearance, receive slight applause.

"*Remporter sa veste;*" to make a *fiasco*.

"*Au rideau,*" is the same cry as our call-boy

makes to the ladies and gentlemen in the green-room. "*Overture on;*" all ready for the first scene.

"*Roccoco;*" the essence of mediocrity, as applied to an actor or a drama; it also applies to an actor who keeps up old-fashioned notions, or to an actress who sets proper costumes at defiance.

"*Ronfler;*" to dwell strongly on the letter R; which is supposed to have great effect in tragedy or melodrama at some provincial theatres.—"Horrible! terrible!! revelation!!!"

"*Tirer la ficelle;*" to sing falsely.

"*Faire du titre;*" to attract curiosity by a flaming play-bill, and to alter and add to the original title of pieces; to which I have already alluded.

"*Tox;*" the lowest slang for a bad piece.

"*Tour de faveur;*" an author cried up by a *coterie;* an actor who, patronized by noble patrons of the drama, succeeds, as an act of favour, in getting a drama in which he has a prominent part brought out at once; a *débutante* who, having "a friend at Court," finds herself in the front rank of dancers, while others, more talented, occupy an inferior place.

"*Trepignements forcés ;*" stamping of feet, either used in a *cabal* against an artist, or as applause to some patriotic or national allusion.

"*Utilités*" answers to our "general utility actors."

"*Vedette ;*" advertising the name of an actor or actress in large letters on the playbills and posters.

Having mentioned the names of "Michot" and "Degazon," it might appear invidious to omit others. I therefore give the names of those who have immortalized themselves by leaving behind a record of the services that raised them to the highest pinnacle of histrionic fame.

"Les Clairval," which include the principal singers of the Opéra Comique; "Les Douzainville," named after an actor who made his *début* at the ancient Opéra Comique; De Louvois, during the second year of the Republic; he subsequently went to the Montansier Theatre, and, at the death of Trisi, to the Favart; "Les Gavudan," or the Talma of the Opera House; "Les Gouthier," named after a celebrated actress, who made her *début* in the year 1778.

This lady was known as La Bonne Gouthier; and well did she merit the title from the *bonhomie* of her acting and the originality of her manner. Her principal characters were the Nurse in "Fanfan and Colas;" Mathurine in "Blaise and Babet;" Ma Tante Aurore; Babet in "Philippe and Georgette." Of her it was said, "She knew how to make you laugh or cry." As Ma Tante Aurore Madame Gouthier was inimitable. In French, what the Honourable Mrs. Wrottesley is in English.

Here I am reminded of some very clever epigrammatic criticisms upon plays that have constantly found their way into the French newspapers. For instance: when a piece entitled "Monsieur Jacques" was produced at one of the Parisian theatres, and unequivocally condemned—I might use a stronger and more familiar English term—the following laconic notice appeared:—

"'Monsieur Jacques,' a paru et disparu."

Again when "Moirond et Compagnie" was first represented at the Gymnase the *Chronique* thus described it:—

"Prenez 'La Femme à Deux Maris,' jetez-y 'L'Homme Gris,' assaisonnez ce mélange avec une dose eventée du Chrysale des 'Femmes Savantes,' et servez froid: vous aurez 'Moirond et Compagnie.'"

Another witticism suggests itself to me. A French writer, under the *nom de plume* of Pirouette, contributes the following *jeu d'esprit* to the *Tintamarre*:—

"Les frères Coquelin, avant d'être comédiens, étaient patissiers; leurs travaux étaient déja excessivement *tartistiques*."

The following grants were voted in 1834 to the Parisian theatres. What they are at the present moment I am unable to ascertain.

	Francs.
Grand Opera	670,000
Pensions of retired Artists	180,000
	———850,000
Théâtre Français	34,000
Opéra Comique	7,200
Italian Opera	2,800

The curtain is about to be lowered on my imperfect drama, but before it falls I wish to follow the old-established custom of giving it (what, in theatrical parlance, is called) a "tag." With regard to the foreign artists, my object has been to

"Conservez à chacun son propre caractère,"

for true it is

"La nature, féconde en bizarres portraits,
Dans chaque âme est marquée à différens traits."

Also to do justice to a nation which "a toujours été vive, gaie, brave, et généreuse."

For myself I would say with Shakespeare:

FALL OF THE CURTAIN.

"Thus far with rough and all unable pen,
　Our bending author hath pursu'd the story;
　In little room confining mighty men;
　Mangling by starts the full course of their glory.
　Small time, but, in that small, most greatly liv'd
　The Stars of England."

. . . .

"So on your patience evermore attending,
　Now joy wait on you! Here our play has ended."

EXEUNT OMNES.

THE END.

www.ingramcontent.com/pod-product-compliance
Lightning Source LLC
Chambersburg PA
CBHW031945230426
43672CB00010B/2053